THE GIRL BEHIND THE CHAIR

From Rags to Riches to Redemption

THE GIRL BEHIND THE CHAIR

From Rags to Riches to Redemption

CINDY HUNT

The Girl Behind the Chair
Copyright © 2025 by Cindy Hunt
First Paperback Edition: December 2025

Unless otherwise noted, Scripture quotations are taken from The Holy Bible, New International Version® NIV® Copyright © 1973, 1978, 1984, 2011 by Biblica, Inc. Used with permission. All rights reserved worldwide. Scripture quotations marked (CSB) have been taken from the CHRISTIAN STANDARD BIBLE®, Copyright © 2017 by Holman Bible Publishers. Used by permission. Christian Standard Bible® and CSB® are federally registered trademarks of Holman Bible Publishers. Scripture quotations marked (ESV) are from the ESV® Bible (The Holy Bible, English Standard Version®), © 2001 by Crossway, a publishing ministry of Good News Publishers. Text Edition: 2016. Used by permission. All rights reserved. Scripture quotations marked (NKJV) are from the HOLY BIBLE, NEW KING JAMES VERSION (NKJV). Copyright © 1982 by Thomas Nelson Publishers. Used by permission. All rights reserved. Scripture quotations marked (NLT) are taken from the Holy Bible, New Living Translation, copyright © 1996, 2004, 2015 by Tyndale House Foundation. Used by permission of Tyndale House Publishers, Inc., Carol Stream, Illinois 60188. All rights reserved.

To order products, or for any other correspondence, contact:

KINGDOM BRIDGES
PUBLISHING

Kingdom Bridges Publishing
78 Folly Rd. Blvd. B9–1135
Charleston, SC 29407
www.kingdombn.com/publishing
Tel.: 843-732-9377
E-mail: admin@kingdombn.com
Or reach us on Facebook & Instagram @kingdombridgespublishing

Chief Editor: Julie A. Weigel
Book cover design: Kingdom Bridges Publishing in Collaboration with West Word Paradox

ISBN: 979-8-9932193-1-8

Printed in the United States of America.
Library of Congress data is available for this title.

Cindy is a radiant voice of encouragement whose joy lights up every room she enters. Walking expertly in the gift of exhortation, she inspires others to encounter God's love in a real and tangible way. A devoted student of Scripture, she delves deeply into the Word and honors it as the guiding compass of her life. Having overcome a difficult childhood, Cindy has allowed the Lord to heal, grow, and shape her into a powerful vessel of hope. Led daily by the Holy Spirit, she carries God's presence into ordinary moments, making His goodness unmistakably manifest. Her heart is to uplift, strengthen, and point people toward the boundless grace that transformed her story.

Peggy Thibodeau
Deeper Water Ministries
Facebook @Peggy.Thibodeau

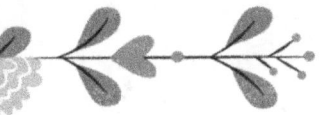

Dedication

F OR MY SISTER, BETTY HUNT COOPER—Though you have passed from this world into the presence of our Lord, the strength and love you poured into my life remain. You were my rock when I was unsteady, my confidante and closest friend, the voice that cheered me on when the world fell silent. Your love was constant, your faith in me unshaken, and your example still inspires me to press on. Until we meet again in heaven, you are always loved and never forgotten.

Table of Contents

$$\longrightarrow\!\!\!\ggg\!\!\!\ggg\!\!-\!\!\lll\!\!\!\lll\!\!\longleftarrow$$

—⟩⟩⟩⟩⟩⟩—⟨⟨⟨⟨⟨—

# Acknowledgements

I AM DEEPLY INDEBTED TO the men and women God used to shape, heal, and guide me on this journey. Each of you has left an eternal imprint on my life, and this book would not exist without the ways you poured into me.

To Matt Green—your influence on my life has been more profound than that of any other teacher. I have been blessed by many men and women of God who taught me His ways, and I hold deep respect for each of them. Yet what you carried reached deeper. Through you, the Scriptures came alive in a way I had never known before. You didn't just teach me the Word—you breathed life into it, and in doing so, you breathed life into me. For that, I will always be grateful.

To Jim and Marianne Wright—your obedience to the Lord in preparing a room for me in your home became one of the greatest gifts of my life. In that sacred space, God began the deep healing of my heart. Through your one-on-one ministry and the love you poured into me, I learned the difference between knowing truth in my head and allowing it to speak to my heart. It was there that deliverance and restoration took root in ways I would never have known otherwise. I am forever grateful.

To Cindy Riley—though your name doesn't appear in this book, it would take an entire volume to tell our story together. Still, I cannot let this pass without acknowledging you. Without your influence— the iron sharpening iron, the steadfast example of walking by faith and trusting in God's provision—I would not be who I am today. You helped me lay down self-sufficiency and lean wholly on Him. For that, I am eternally thankful.

To Pastor Al Brice of Covenant Love Church—thank you for believing in me and supporting me as a missionary to the nations. Your covering, encouragement, and prayers have been a source of strength through the years. I remain deeply grateful for your investment in my life and calling.

To Pastor Dan Krawchuck—I thank God for the season I spent under your ministry, where I grew spiritually and learned to walk by the Spirit. I carry in my heart the prophetic word you spoke—that the Lord has given me the master key—and I have witnessed Him supernaturally open doors no human effort could have unlocked. Thank you for your faithfulness to our Lord and King. I will always be your "Sunshine."

To Aileen Murphy—my dearest friend, you're a sharp cookie who always shoots from the hip. When I need honesty, you give it straight; when I need encouragement, you're right there. You keep me laughing, you keep me grounded, and you remind me who I am—even when you call me "Mrs. Ripp." You are the truest and best kind of friend, and I treasure the gift of your steadfast presence in my life.

To my children: Little D. and Jatana—this is your story as much as it is mine, your legacy written through the pages of my life. My prayer is that it will continue through you and your children, carrying forward the lessons, the love, and the faith that God has woven into our family. I love you more than words could ever say.

Introduction

Dear Reader,

Every one of us carries stories we do not tell. Some are buried so deeply we convince ourselves they no longer matter. Others we carry on the surface, hidden behind smiles and strength, while inside we ache. I know this because it had been my life.

I was born into hardship as a Lumbee Indian child, the youngest of seven, shaped by trauma long before I had words for it. I thought I could outrun the pain by building a life of my own—marriage, children, responsibilities—but what I did not see was how the brokenness in me spilled into the lives of those I loved most.

Maybe you know that feeling: the quiet realization that what hurt you has a way of hurting others, even when you never meant for it to. For years I searched for healing in the places that looked holy. I surrendered to the Lord, served on the mission field, gave my life to helping others. I believed that if I just did enough, gave enough, obeyed enough, I would be free. But I discovered something I had missed all along: you can do all the right things, even good and godly things, and still not be healed.

Why? Because true healing doesn't come from what we do for God. *It comes when we allow Him to reach into the hidden places of our hearts*—the places we protect, bury, or avoid—and bring His light there.

As you read these pages, you may find yourself wondering: Could this all have possibly happened to one woman? The answer is, yes. Every chapter you will read is not just a story; it is a piece of my soul, torn apart and scattered, now gathered back together by the hand of God.

This book is not just my story. It is an invitation. As you turn these pages, if you catch glimpses of your own journey, I pray you will allow God to uncover what has been hidden in you—not to bring shame, but to bring freedom. Because the truth is this: *only when the heart is healed can we live the life we were created to live.*

My prayer is that, through my story, you will begin to see your own in a new way—not as something to hide, but as something God can redeem.

With hope,

Cindy Hunt

A Fragile Beginning, A Greater Purpose

THE SMELL OF ANTISEPTIC CLUNG to the hospital room on a hot summer day in July 1952. Harsh white lights glared overhead. Nurses rushed past as my mother lay fighting for her life—her appendix ruptured, her body slipping toward death. My father stood silently beside her, overwhelmed and helpless.

A doctor pulled him aside. "We may be able to save one—your wife or the baby?" Without hesitation my father chose her. But heaven had better plans.

I arrived weighing barely over two pounds—a whisper of life wrapped in hospital linen and wires. The machines hummed around me. For two months I lay in an incubator, my fragile chest rising and falling with effort, each breath a small miracle.

When they finally brought me home several months later, I was so tiny I didn't fit in a crib. Instead, they laid me in a dresser drawer lined with soft blankets. My sister Betty, still a little girl herself, took me in her arms like a babydoll. She fed me, changed me, and carried me from room to room as if she'd been born for it.

Before I turned a year old, our family packed up to leave Temple, Texas. My parents longed to return to my father's hometown of

Lumberton, North Carolina. We had little to carry, just one another, and all of us crowded into the car for the long drive east. Somewhere between miles and exhaustion, my father picked up a hitchhiker to share the driving. On a long stretch over the Mississippi River, that stranger nodded off behind the wheel. The car veered suddenly and plunged off the road, tumbling down an embankment.

I was thrown from the vehicle.

Panic rose as my parents scrambled through the wreckage. I can only imagine my mother's scream, my father's dread. They searched the brush and the riverbank, terrified that I had been swept into the water. Then they found me—bruised, battered, but alive. My tiny body lay nestled in a patch of bushes, miraculously spared.

Whenever I picture that moment, I don't see chaos—I see baby Moses, drifting through the reeds of the Nile, held by a purpose even he couldn't understand. Twice, God had intervened on my behalf: once in the silence of an incubator and again on the muddy banks of the Mississippi. And though I didn't know it then, He was writing a story—*mine*.

Lumberton did not welcome us. We were poor. We were Lumbee. And in that town, being Native meant being invisible.

There were no programs to help us, no one looking out for families like mine. Prejudice wasn't hidden—it shaped where we could live, what jobs we could have, and how people looked at us.

Our house sat on the edge of everything—town, society, even hope. Wind slid through the cracks in the walls. The floor creaked under our bare feet. The cold wasn't just outside; it lived with us. But worse than the cold was the emptiness. There was no warmth. No consistent care. Just noise—parties, drinking, and disappearances.

Lumberton was a dry town, but liquor flowed anyway, smuggled through back doors and bootleg routes. My parents knew where to find it. They chased escape in bottles while we chased safety in silence. We were children raising ourselves. And in the middle of the mess, Betty, still only a child herself, became our shelter. When our parents vanished into long nights of drinking, Betty filled the gap. She cooked with scraps, turned nothing into dinner, and when there was truly nothing left, walked barefoot to our neighbors' homes and asked for help.

I can still see her—skinny and brave, standing on someone's porch with her chin held high enough to stay strong yet low enough to stay respectful. She was our stand-in mother. Our protector. Jesus' hands and feet in a house that had forgotten what love looked like. For her, there existed no thank-yous, no recognition—only quiet strength. She carried the weight of our family on her small shoulders, never wavering, never asking for anything in return.

As I reflect on my past, the promise of Psalm 27:10 brings comfort, *"Though my father and mother forsake me, the Lord will receive me."* And through Betty, he did—though I didn't understand it then, looking back I can see how God's hand was quietly guiding, protecting, and watching over me every step of the way.

✳ · ✳ · ✳

When I was about six years old, we moved again—this time to Fayetteville, where my father found work cutting soldiers' hair at Fort Bragg. Our new house sat on the poorest edge of town. Faded siding. A musty odor. Rats in the walls. But even that wasn't the worst of it. The worst came at night.

The slow, heavy sound of my father's footsteps coming down the hall. I would lie frozen under my thin blanket, barely breathing, waiting to see whose room he would enter. Most nights, he passed me by.

But one night, he didn't. His hand slipped beneath the covers and into my panties. I stopped breathing; my body turned to stone.

"Daddy?" I whispered.

There was no answer. My blanket—once my shield—offered no protection now. I wanted so badly to disappear into the floor. I didn't understand what was happening. I just knew everything was wrong.

That night changed me. Fear became a shadow that never left. I began to shrink from voices, from footsteps, and even from kindness. The voice that should have comforted me, the footsteps that should have brought safety, the hand that should have shown love and tenderness—all of it now filled me with fear. And if he could betray me, anyone else could too. I didn't know who was safe anymore.

Except for Betty.

✳ · ✳ · ✳

My Hiding Place

In the corner of the living room sat a worn-out plaid chair. To most, it was just old furniture. To me, it became a sanctuary. I would crawl behind it, knees tucked into my chest, the smell of dust in my nose. I'd stay hidden there for hours, silent, unseen. That chair caught my tears, held my breath, and shielded me from a world I couldn't name.

We were three sisters, and each of us was touched by the same hands. But Betty—Betty bore the worst of it. Abuse in childhood leaves wounds no one can see, but they echo through everything. It tells you to be quiet. To be small. To doubt your worth. It poisons the way you love, trust, and dream. And it doesn't stay in childhood—it chases you into adulthood unless Truth breaks the silence.

I may never know what broke my father, but I do know this: the cycle stopped with me. I do not tell this story to stay in the pain, but to pull someone else out of it. Healing is possible, and sometimes the first step is speaking the truth out loud.

Chapter 2

Fractured Family

I USED TO THINK OUR FAMILY WAS like any other—maybe a little rough around the edges, but nothing a few apologies or holidays couldn't patch over. Just cracks. The kind you learn to step around. But as I got older, I realized—ours wasn't just cracked. It was fractured—deep, sharp, generational.

The dirt was red in Lumberton, North Carolina. It clung to bare feet and tobacco roots the same way pain clung to the men in my father's family. My father, Hector Hunt, was just a boy when he left school in third grade and joined his brothers in the fields, their hands blistered from work that paid almost nothing. He never talked much about his childhood, but it showed—in the way he moved, the way he clenched his jaw when money was tight, and the way he drank.

His family was Lumbee—proud, Native, and poor. And though Lumberton was full of others just like them, it didn't protect them from prejudice. The systems worked against them. Opportunities passed them by. And somewhere in all that injustice, the bottle became their comfort. My father lost a brother to it—shot in a drunken brawl, right there in the dirt they'd all grown up on.

But my father was handsome. The kind of man who turned heads, with sharp cheekbones, thick black hair, and eyes that didn't give much away. Maybe that's what drew my mother to him. Gladys

Maynor was also Lumbee, raised in the backroads of Dunn, North Carolina. Her life was marked by poverty too, but also by frailty. She was sick more often than well. Her body had been pushed too hard, too long—too many children, not enough rest, and dreams that never had room to grow. When the two of them came together, it wasn't out of healing. It was survival. And survival doesn't always make love.

Charles was the firstborn. Then Betty. They came before the war, before Korea took my father away for two years. While he was gone, my mother gave birth to two more children—Lloyd and Diane. They weren't his. With no money, no help, and no strength left, she handed them over to be raised by someone else. Then came Welford, another child not fathered by the man whose name we carried.

By the time my father came home from the war, the family had already grown without him. Still, they tried to stitch things back together. Gary came next, and then me—the final child in a long line of complicated beginnings. We didn't talk about the past in our house. We didn't ask who belonged to who. But we all felt it—this undercurrent of shame that made us walk on tiptoes around certain names, around certain years.

Lloyd was never mentioned—not until I was in high school. His name dropped like a secret no one meant to say. I had a brother? I remember the ache of that discovery—how a person could be your blood, your story, and still be erased. Diane and Welford eventually came back to us, but Lloyd remained a ghost.

I met him once. And then he died.

He was in his early twenties, playing a reckless game of chicken—sitting in a car on train tracks with his girlfriend. The train didn't stop. The car didn't move. They both lost.

Diane's death came soon after. She was pumping gas, leaning between two cars when one rolled forward and crushed her in an instant. She died in our mother's arms.

Welford lasted longer, but the pain inside him never let up. He drank, he used, he spiraled. There were moments of light—glimpses of the brother he could've been—but the darkness always pulled him back.

One by one, they slipped through our fingers—three lives lost before they had a chance to be lived. Sometimes I wonder if their fates were sealed by choices that were never theirs to make: a mother too weary to mother, a father too broken to protect, a world that never welcomed children like us with open arms. Choices that carried consequences none of us could escape.

But even then, God never turned away. Even in the silence. Even in addiction. Even in the chaos and loss—He saw them. He wept with them. He waited for them.

"Whoever sows injustice reaps calamity." —Proverbs 22:8

I've seen it with my own eyes. When bitterness is sown, bitterness grows. When children are neglected, they carry that pain and emptiness into every room they enter for the rest of their lives. Pain, when left untouched, doesn't die—it passes on. But so does mercy. So does healing. So does grace. Because when God is invited into even the most broken soil, something new can bloom.

Chapter 3

Family Was All We Had

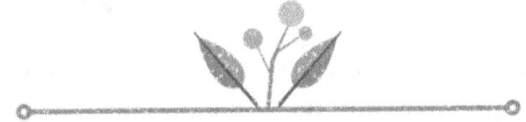

THE PINE NEEDLES CRUNCHED under our bare feet as my brother, Gary, and I made our way through the woods. We weren't just walking—we were on a mission. Past the tall trees, through the smell of sap and sun-warmed dirt, awaited Aunt Gussie's house. She was one of my father's sisters, but with her we felt something different—safe, cared for, even loved. That little trail wasn't just a path through the woods; it was the way to comfort, the place where we could finally breathe. Her door was always open. Not just literally, but spiritually. We didn't have to knock. We didn't even have to speak. One look from her soft brown eyes, and we knew—we mattered.

Aunt Gussie didn't raise her voice. She didn't preach. But when she folded her hands and bowed her head at the kitchen table, something holy entered the room. She was the first person I ever saw live out the quiet strength of faith. Long before I understood who God was, I felt His presence in her kitchen, in her garden, and in her arms.

Sunday mornings meant church, and Aunt Gussie would take us to Saddle Tree Church of God. It was small with wooden pews, creaky floors, and windows that let in more light than air, but when the saints began to sing, it felt like heaven itself cracked open. I didn't always understand the preaching, but I understood the power. It was joy—raw and real. And after church? Dinner followed on the grounds.

Long tables were set up under the trees and covered in the likes of fried chicken, cornbread, and banana pudding. We'd grab paper plates and run barefoot through the grass, tasting food that felt like a miracle. Children like us, who knew the ache of empty cupboards, suddenly found our bellies full and our hearts lifted.

Then the music would start. Quartets stood shoulder to shoulder and let their voices fly. Songs about Jesus, redemption, and heaven's promise echoed across the field. I didn't know the lyrics, but I knew the longing. Those harmonies planted something in me—something eternal.

Aunt Gussie was a praying woman—her whispers to Heaven rose constantly, as natural as breathing. And because her faith in God was deep and unwavering, I believe He heard every one. It was through her prayers, through her quiet example, that God first began to show Himself to me. In her faith, the beginnings of my own were planted.

$$* \cdot * \cdot *$$

My father's other sister, Aunt Big Bell, lived in Lumberton. Her house sat crooked on a patch of dusty land, the wood gray with age and the porch boards soft underfoot. There was no indoor plumbing, just a pump out back and an outhouse that creaked when you pulled the door. Spiders claimed the corners, and the wooden seat always seemed colder than the wind. But inside that worn shack was life— loud, messy, and unforgettable as it was.

"Y'all get out there, and catch me a chicken!" Aunt Big Bell's voice boomed from the kitchen. Her apron was stained with flour, and her arms were folded like she meant business.

We did not hesitate. Barefoot and wild, we tore across the yard, laughing and stumbling after a squawking blur of feathers. The chickens darted between our legs, wings flapping, dust flying.

Catching one was part chase, part miracle. When we finally captured the chosen one, we carried it like a trophy back to Aunt Big Bell.

She didn't flinch. One snap of the neck, one dip in boiling water, and the plucking began. I watched with wide eyes—half fascinated, half horrified. It was life—raw and unfiltered. When that chicken hit the hot grease, the smell of Aunt Big Bell's fried chicken alone made the day worth it. Nothing in the world tasted like that.

As the food cooked, the house filled with more aunts, more cousins, and more laughter. Aunt Irene brought her kids, and sometimes Aunt Gussie would come, too. The women played penny poker at the kitchen table, slapping cards and clinking bottles while shouting over one another like a family choir.

We kids stayed outside until the sun began to fall, turning sticks into swords and dirt into kingdoms. When we came inside, the table was a patchwork of cast iron and cracked dishes, stacked high with love and grease and garden-grown blessings.

I don't remember my mother bringing anything, but no one said a word. The aunts just filled our plates, like love didn't keep score.

✳ · ✳ · ✳

Then there was the town where my mother's people came from. Visiting them felt different. Quieter. Heavier. Her people lived behind drawn curtains and thin smiles. We weren't close. Not really. Not the way we were with our cousins in Lumberton.

One Sunday, we were invited to eat at my mother's brother's home. It was a small house, humble, stretched thin by poverty. I found out later that my aunt had sold her iron just to afford the meal. She had wanted to appear generous, but desperation laced every corner of that day.

As we sat down at the table, I noticed the children—my cousins—weren't there. I looked around, confused. Then I saw them outside, their faces pressed to the windows, watching us eat. They weren't allowed to join us. Not even to come inside.

Something broke in me that day. I didn't understand pride, or shame, or survival—but I understood wrong. There was no joy in that meal. No laughter, no light. Just a heavy silence that followed me home.

But not all memories are bruises.

My mother's sister, Aunt Little Bell, lived in Fayetteville, North Carolina. Her family was different. Their house was noisy, joyful, and chaotic. Our cousins weren't just relatives—they were our best friends. We fought and forgave like siblings. We shared food, secrets, and stories. We were poor, but we were close. And that closeness was wealth.

There were days I didn't know if I was safe, or seen, or wanted. But then came Sundays at Aunt Gussie's, or laughter in Aunt Big Bell's yard, or games with cousins in Aunt Little Bell's house. Those were the bright spots. The warmth in the cold. The giggles between the grief. The taste of grace in a house with no running water. Family didn't fix everything, but in those moments—it was everything we had.

And through it all, God was near—quietly stitching hope through fried chicken, gospel music, and the prayers of a woman who never stopped believing. In the middle of brokenness, He wove ordinary moments into threads of grace, showing me that even the smallest acts of love revealed that He saw me, cared for me, and loved me.

Chapter 4

Out of Place

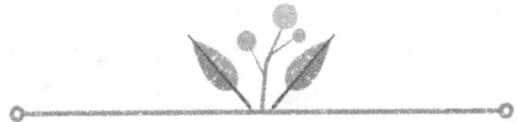

THERE'S A MOMENT IN LIFE when the world suddenly feels bigger—and colder. For me, that moment came when I left the safety of the Indian school and stepped into a world that didn't know what to do with me.

At Les Maxwell, an Indian school with every grade under one roof, I was just one of the kids. Brown-skinned, barefoot in the summer, surrounded by cousins who knew my name and shared my world. We didn't have much, but we had each other. School was simple. Familiar. Safe. Everyone knew who we were—and more importantly, they knew what we were.

Then came integration. They called it progress. A step forward. A better opportunity. But it didn't feel like an opportunity. It felt like exile. Suddenly, I was in a white school. The building looked different, smelled different, and felt different. The kids stared, and the teachers judged. No one said it out loud, but I knew—I didn't belong. The segregation was sharp at first—felt in glances, whispered comments, and the quiet distance between us and everyone else. Over time, some of that tension softened. Small connections were made, a few friendships formed, and the edges of exclusion became slightly less harsh, though the memory of being an outsider never fully faded.

In 1964, when I was about twelve years old, we moved into a white neighborhood, establishing a home base in a nice brick house on a quiet street with trimmed lawns and clean sidewalks. On the outside, it looked like we had arrived. Like *The Jeffersons*, we were "moving on up." But inside, everything was changing. Gone were the dusty roads and barefoot cousins. Gone were the loud dinners at Aunt Gussie's house—the laughter, the music, the closeness. In their place were closed doors, quiet stares, and a neighborhood where no one came to visit. The children didn't ask us to play. The mothers didn't stop by to chat. We were watched, but never welcomed. And school? That was its own world. I was no longer surrounded by people who shared my name, my story, or my skin. No one knew who I was, and no one wanted to.

And while I was navigating this strange new space, my body was changing too. I knew I needed a bra. I felt it with every movement. Normally, a girl would ask her mother about these things, but my mother was rarely present—working different jobs, emotionally distant, and often too tired or preoccupied to truly mother me. Betty was grown and acted as a stand-in mother at times, but even she couldn't give permission for the things my father controlled. But when I asked my father, he dismissed me. "You don't need that yet," he said, as if my body should wait for his approval. So instead of a bra, I wore one of my brother's old T-shirts under my clothes—thick, shapeless, and humiliating. I knew the other kids noticed. The girls looked. The boys laughed. I already stood out for my skin and my silence—now I stood out even more.

My emotions were shifting. My sense of self was unraveling. I didn't have the words for it back then, but now I know—I was grieving. Grieving the loss of familiarity. Of comfort. Of identity. I had gone from being seen and known to being watched and dismissed. I was too Indian to be White. Too quiet to be heard. Too unsure to speak. Everything around me was changing, and I wasn't ready.

Yet even as everything shifted around me, I held onto one bright memory—our first Christmas in that new house. That Christmas was different. It was magical. For once, everything seemed to fall into place, and it felt like what I imagined "normal families" must feel at Christmastime. Laughter echoed through every room, and the house itself seemed to smile with us. The kitchen overflowed with the scent of sweet pies and rich cakes, and my father—of all people—bustled about like the head chef of his own little holiday bakery. Cinnamon, vanilla, sugar—it was unforgettable.

The record player spun "Rockin' Around the Christmas Tree," and the living room transformed into a stage. My siblings and I danced like we were on television—and then, something even more unexpected happened: our parents joined in! My father, apron and all, danced in the middle of the room, pies cooling on the counter, my mother clapping along to the beat. At that moment, my mother and father weren't burdened or broken. They were just people—laughing, dancing, alive.

That year, I got a pair of white go-go boots. I felt like the coolest girl in the world. I stomped and twirled like I was on *American Bandstand*, my siblings cheering me on. Gary had saved up to buy Betty a whole case of Mountain Dew—her favorite—and when he gave it to her, it was like he was handing over treasure. The way she hugged him, you'd think it was gold. We all had something that night—new clothes, sweet soda, shiny boots—and for a few bright hours, we weren't poor. We weren't outsiders. We were just *happy*.

By the time we moved into that home in the white neighborhood, Charles had graduated from Les Maxwell and joined the Army. Betty had become a hairdresser—both of them carving out paths the best they could with the little foundation they'd been given. That left Welford, Diane, Gary, and me to navigate the new school system.

Welford and Diane were in high school, already trying to stay afloat, while Gary and I were still in elementary school—young enough to be confused, but old enough to feel the weight of it. By the time I reached middle school, the gap had only grown wider.

The shift was brutal.

The white schools weren't built to help us catch up. They were built to leave us behind. At Les Maxwell, we'd had teachers who cared, but they were under-resourced and overburdened. We learned what we could with what they had. But the truth was—we were already behind when we stepped into those new classrooms. And it showed.

Welford and Diane started skipping school more days than they attended. The shame of not understanding—of sitting in rooms where they couldn't keep up—was too much. The teachers didn't offer help. No one checked in. No one asked why. They just assumed we didn't care. But we did. We just didn't know how to run a race we hadn't been trained for.

All I really remember from that first year in the new school was how alone I felt. I didn't have a single friend. What I had were boys who teased me—about my skin, my clothes, my quietness. They made me feel small. Unworthy. Out of place.

So I made a silent vow, deep down inside: one day, I would get even. Not with fists. Not with anger. But by becoming someone. Someone they'd have to notice. Someone they couldn't ignore or dismiss.

At the time, I didn't know what that meant. I just imagined being respected. Successful. Seen.

At home, we created our own joy. Simple joy. It was just us kids, a record player, and the living room rug. Welford, Diane, Gary, and I would throw the rug back like it was a stage curtain, crank up the music, and dance like nobody was watching. For those few minutes, we weren't struggling Indian kids from the wrong side of town—we were performers—*Stars.* We laughed and spun and forgot how hard the world outside could be.

But the truth still found us.

I failed my first year in the new school. There's no gentle way to say it. I struggled—badly. The teachers talked too fast. The books felt foreign. The expectations were different. And the loneliness was crushing. So I failed. I had to repeat the seventh grade. At the time, it felt like the ultimate shame. But looking back now, I see it differently—I was never given a fair start. None of us were.

Welford and Diane didn't even make it that far. They started skipping school so often that eventually they just stopped going. It wasn't rebellion—not really. It was exhaustion. It was walking into a place every day where no one expected you to succeed—and finally believing it. They were smart. But they were tired. Tired of being behind. Tired of being stared at. Tired of pretending to fit into a system that never had a place for them.

The school didn't lose them. It never had them to begin with.

And though our surroundings had changed, our home life hadn't. We might have lived in a nicer house, on a quieter street, in a "better" neighborhood—but the struggle inside the walls remained the same. There was no encouragement. No help with homework. No praise for trying. No support when we failed. We were expected to adapt. To rise. To figure it out on our own—while carrying the weight of poverty, silence, and shame on our backs. It was too heavy for children to bear. But we bore it anyway.

Although Welford and Diane quit and I failed, something in me held on. Maybe it was stubbornness. Maybe it was that promise I made to myself when those boys laughed—that I would become someone they couldn't ignore. At the time, I didn't know who that someone would be.

But I knew this: I wouldn't give up. Even when I was out of place. Even when I was unseen. I was determined to keep going. I didn't know where that road would take me—but I knew I was going to keep walking.

And unbeknownst to me, an unseen Hand was there the whole time—helping me, guiding me, strengthening me, especially when life got even harder.

Chapter 5

Room to Grow, Nowhere to Go

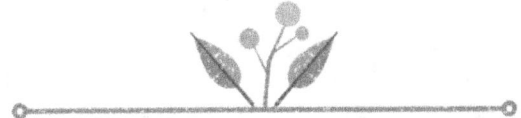

T HAT BRICK HOUSE IN THE white neighborhood looked like a promise—a new neighborhood,. paved streets, and lawns trimmed clean. The kind of place where, from the outside, it seemed like we had finally stepped into something better—and maybe safer.

But a new house doesn't change old truths.

Our address had changed, but the fear inside our home hadn't. My father was still who he had always been. My mother remained a shadow—fading in the background. And I was still the shy, quiet girl, trying to keep up with a world growing faster than I was ready for.

I started to find new faces—Jody Ward, a girl from the neighborhood, became one of my first real friends. So did the York family next door. They had three children—two boys and a girl— close in age to Welford, Diane, Gary, and me. We didn't have much, but we had each other. At least sometimes.

Still, the rules in our home hadn't softened—if anything, they had tightened. We had a bigger yard now, but we weren't free to run in it—space doesn't always mean freedom. We had room to grow. But nowhere to go—my father made sure of that. Even in a nicer house, even in a nicer neighborhood, I still found myself hiding behind the chair—because fear doesn't care where you live.

The four of us—Welford, Diane, Gary, and I—shared a bond only siblings raised in survival can understand. We laughed together, hid secrets, and carried one another's pain in silence. But we also fought, pushed, and sometimes hurt each other in ways no one on the outside could see.

Welford, Diane, and Gary had started testing the edges of our world. They were older, braver, bolder. They skipped school often—sometimes disappearing for the entire day and slipping back in just before our parents returned. They weren't just curious. They were restless. Rebellious. Wild in ways I didn't yet understand.

I was still the timid one—still trying to stay in line, even though the line kept moving. But I wanted to belong. I wanted my siblings to see me. So one day, when Diane and Welford convinced me to skip school with them, I did.

My chest pounded the whole time. My face was hot with fear. We hid out in the woods for hours, waiting until we were sure our parents were gone before sneaking back into the house like nothing had happened.

That day marked a shift—not loud or dramatic, but slow and quiet, like a crack forming under the surface. I wanted to be accepted by them. But deep down, I knew I wasn't made of the same fire. Or maybe I just knew the cost—and I wasn't willing to pay it. Because in our house, stepping out of line always came with a price—and it was almost always paid in bruises.

Behind the house sat a small shed—just big enough to fit a couple of beds and not much else. It wasn't insulated. No heat. No air conditioning. Just old wood and emptiness. But somehow, it became part of our living space. Sometimes it was a bedroom—used by Welford and Gary, or Diane and me, depending on the season and the mood inside the house.

That shed was its own little world. Just far enough from the house to feel like freedom, but close enough to still hear the echoes of everything we were trying to escape.

It was also a hiding place. A place where things could happen that didn't belong in the light. And it's where something strange began—I started sniffing gasoline.

There were always old cans out there, the scent of chemicals lingering in the air. At first, it was just passing by. Then leaning in. Then breathing deep—on purpose. I loved the smell. The rush. The way the world seemed to fade at the edges. Sometimes I would sniff until I felt lightheaded. Sometimes until I passed out.

It sounds foolish now. Reckless. Dangerous. But back then, it was just another way to escape. To forget. To deal with the pain and trauma that no child should ever have to endure. My body had learned how to bear the pain. But my mind? It needed a place to go.

And in that shed, gasoline became my escape hatch. I didn't think about the science. I didn't know it at the time, but sniffing gasoline could have destroyed my brain, my lungs—my life. But I was just a child, trying to make sense of pain with no voice and no help. I just knew it made me feel less. Less fear. Less hurt. Less everything.

Even now, I don't fully understand why I survived it. But I believe God protected me. Even when I couldn't protect myself. Even when the people who were supposed to watch over me didn't. Even when I had no idea what I was doing to my body or mind—*He knew.*

God saw me. He watched over that little shed. Over the girl no one else noticed—hiding behind chairs, behind fear, behind fumes. And He kept His hand on me, as Psalm 91:11 promises, *"For He will command His angels concerning you to guard you in all your ways."*

I believe He did. I didn't know His name the way I do now. I didn't yet understand His love. But I know He was there. Because I survived things that should have broken me.

And that shed? It wasn't just a hiding place. It became holy ground. A place where God hovered close—silent, unseen, but never absent.

Not every memory from the shed was about escape. Some were about childhood—or at least the parts of it we tried to salvage. We didn't have playgrounds or toys. We had dirt and sticks, old bikes, and whatever our imaginations could turn into fun.

When the mood in our house was light enough—or the grown-ups were distracted—we ran wild in our yard with the Yorks, chasing each other until the sun dipped behind the trees.

One day, we were playing like that—laughing, free for a moment. Ben York was chasing me, and I darted toward the shed, giggling as I ran. I slammed the door behind me and leaned against it, trying to catch my breath.

What I didn't realize was that the door had a glass pane. Ben, running full speed, didn't see it—or didn't stop in time. His hand went straight through the glass.

Everything stopped.

There was blood. Glass everywhere. A shard cut me near the eye. It wasn't deep enough to blind me, but it was close. And terrifying. But not just because of the injury. I wasn't afraid of the pain—I was afraid of what my father would do when he found out. That was the worst part of being a child in that house—accidents weren't just painful. They were punishable. Even when it wasn't your fault, you felt guilty. Even when you were bleeding, your first instinct was to hide.

Looking back, it's hard to separate childhood from survival. I was growing, yes—but mostly in silence, mostly in hiding. Danger didn't wear a stranger's face. It lived under our roof. So I found places to disappear. Behind walls. Behind quiet. Inside myself.

But even there—in the silence I wrapped around my pain—I wasn't alone. I didn't have words to pray. But somehow, I knew—something, or *Someone* bigger than me was there. And even then, something deep inside me believed: *I was meant for more than just making it through.*

Chapter 6

Through the Fence

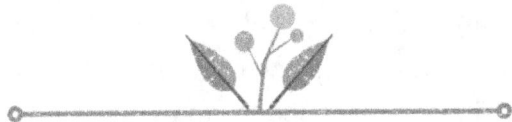

BECOMING A TEENAGER IS SUPPOSED TO feel like stepping into something new—freedom, growth, possibility. For me, it felt like stepping deeper into confinement.

As my body was changing, so were my thoughts and my questions. The world outside our home was shifting too—more cars on the road, new faces in the neighborhood, high school girls with purses and lip gloss and the easy air of belonging.

But inside our house? Nothing changed. If anything, the walls felt tighter. My father's control didn't ease as we grew older—it deepened. His rage didn't fade—it simmered, always just beneath the surface, ready to explode. And we were always bracing for it.

The tension inside the house never eased. It boiled constantly—bubbling under the surface, then erupting without warning. And it didn't just come from my father.

Welford's cruelty had grown sharper, darker. He had always been unpredictable, but now he was full of rage—and I became his target.

He didn't need a reason. Sometimes it was a look. Sometimes it was nothing at all. I lived in fear of him—never knowing when he'd lash out or what might set him off.

So I went back to my old hiding place—behind the chair. The same place I had once used to disappear from my father, I now used to vanish from my brother. The others found their own ways to escape. Welford, Diane, and Gary were always stirring up something.

One day, I came home to find the house in chaos—furniture overturned, drawers pulled out, everything scattered like a storm had swept through. They said someone had broken in. And I believed them. Until I found out it was all a prank. A lie they made up for fun. Until it wasn't fun anymore.

Our parents came home earlier than expected. The story had to hold. My father called the police. The officers walked through the wreckage and gave a glance that said more than words: maybe your boys did this themselves. After all, they were known for skipping school, for causing trouble.

That was all my father needed to hear. He sent us outside—me, Diane, and my mother. Then the beating began. I can still hear it sometimes. The sharp snap of the belt. The screaming. The silence that followed.

But what I remember most is my mother crying. She stood beside us, tears running down her face—but she wasn't crying for both boys. She was crying for Gary—her favorite. The knee baby. The one who had survived polio as a toddler, back when we still lived in Texas.

Betty once told me about it—how, when Gary was just a little boy, she tried to get him dressed. He kept falling, so she popped his legs, thinking he was just being stubborn. But he wasn't. He was sick. He couldn't stand. The house had to be quarantined. And from that moment on, I believe my mother decided Gary was hers to protect.

When Gary was born, my mother told everyone his name was Gary Paul. That's what we all called him. That's who he was to us. But when it came time to sign the birth certificate, my father did what he often did—he took control. He wrote Victor Wayne instead. No discussion. No explanation. No telling anyone. So when Gary started elementary school and the teachers called out "Wayne," he didn't respond. He had no idea who they were talking to.

To them, it was just a name on paper. But to Gary, it was like being erased and rewritten without warning. At home he was Gary Paul, and at school he was Wayne. In between, a boy trying to figure out who he really was. His identity was taken before he had a chance to claim it. In a family where power was everything, even your name— your very self—wasn't always yours to keep.

My father's power didn't always need words; sometimes his silence spoke loudest, shaping who we were and what we dared to be. That control followed us everywhere—until even the boundaries of our own yard bore its mark.

I remember the day the chain-link fence went up. It wrapped around our yard like a warning. He said it was for our protection. But we knew better. It wasn't to keep strangers out—it was to keep us in. That fence didn't just mark the edge of our property. It marked the line we were not allowed to cross. The line between obedience and punishment. Between silence and rebellion.

It happened not long after my cousin Linda came to live with us. She and Diane were close in age, but Linda and I shared something gentler—a quiet closeness built on unspoken understanding. She was a breath of fresh air in a house that so often felt suffocating.

One afternoon, Linda was talking to the young man across the street. He was in the military—kind, respectful, polite. We stood there for only a moment, just talking. Then we heard the car pull up. I'll never forget the sound of the door slamming, or the heavy thud of my father's footsteps. He didn't say a word. He walked straight up and slapped me. Not Linda—me.

Shortly after that, the fence went up. He didn't raise his voice. He didn't need to. The fence was his voice. A chain-link message that said everything we weren't allowed to say. It wasn't just a barrier. It was a boundary. A threat. A warning. A few strands of steel turned our yard into a cage meant to keep us in line.

To keep us locked in. But fences don't just keep people out—they teach you who holds the power. I spent those years learning to live behind barriers. Barriers of control. Barriers of silence. Barriers built by fear and held in place by people who were supposed to love me.

But even behind the fence, God saw me. Even in hiding, He was there. I didn't have the words to pray, but He heard me. I didn't know how to ask for deliverance, but He was already working on it. He allowed me to feel the weight of that pain—not to punish me, but to prepare me. Because healing doesn't begin with pretending. It begins with seeing.

And what I was beginning to see—through the fence, through the pain—was this: I was not forgotten. I was not unloved. I was not meant to stay hidden. God was showing me, even in whispers, that the world was bigger than the fence around me. And the story He was writing for my life was not finished—not even close.

Chapter 7

When I Learned to Fly

GOD SPEAKS IN MANY WAYS—through people, through His still small voice, and sometimes through dreams. For years, I had two recurring dreams that followed me like whispers from another world.

In one, I stood before the house where my father first robbed me of my innocence. It was crumbling—falling down board by board, as if time itself was undoing the damage. And then, in its place, a field of grass. Quiet. Free. I stood there in awe—overwhelmed that something so broken could be undone.

In the other dream, I flew. Sometimes over water, sometimes over buildings, but always upward. I never knew when it would start—I'd just suddenly realize I wasn't walking anymore. And I was never afraid. The fear stayed on the ground. In those moments, I believed I could go anywhere.

These dreams came back to me often during my teenage years when my body was growing but my world was still so small. I wasn't allowed to wear makeup, date boys, or go to school games unless my father came along—and who wanted that? I didn't fit in, and I didn't know how to try.

Cosmetology school was the only bright spot. I started it during my senior year and found it gave me a sense of identity and purpose.

I loved working with my hands—shaping, styling, creating. It was the first time I felt like I had something to offer that was mine and mine alone.

My brother Gary had a girlfriend and seemed determined to carve out a life for himself, despite our father's harshness. My sister Betty had finally escaped—she eloped, claiming her freedom in one bold act of defiance. My cousin Linda married the soldier who lived across the street. Welford eventually drifted further into his own world. And me? I was just waiting. Waiting for graduation. Waiting for my chance to leave.

And then, out of nowhere, Lloyd came back into our lives. My brother—the one I had only heard stories about—was suddenly real. There was a moment, brief but powerful, when I believed we would get the chance to build something. But just as quickly as he came, he was gone again. His life ended tragically on the railroad tracks, and with it, another piece of my heart disappeared. I never really got the chance to know him. Just a flicker of light—and then the darkness returned.

When my junior/senior prom came around, I was shocked my father let me go. I had one date. Just one. I had to be home by 11:00 p.m.—and I was. But that night it felt like something shifted. My dress shimmered in the lights, my hair was perfect, and for a moment, I wasn't the girl hidden behind the fence. I was just Cindy. And that was enough.

That night, and those recurring dreams, whispered the same thing: there's more. There's more than this house, this pain, this fear. There's a world beyond these walls, and I was born to find it.

Looking back, I realize the dreams weren't just a child's imagination—they were prophecies. God was already showing me what was coming: a life of movement, of ministry, of flight. But I also learned something else: when we make vows in fear—vows like "I'll never come back," "I'll never trust again," or "I'll do it all on my own"—those vows can bind us just as tightly as the pain we're trying to escape.

Freedom didn't come the day I left. It came the day I surrendered. Because true freedom isn't found in distance—it's found in Jesus. And when I learned that, I didn't just dream of flying. I finally did.

Chapter 8

The Price of Escape

MY FATHER LEFT FORT BRAGG to open his own barber shop with my brother Charles, in 1970. Betty opened her own salon in the same shopping center, and my mother started a daycare center in a house just behind it. I got a job at the dry cleaners right next door to my father's shop. Maybe he allowed me to work there because he could still keep an eye on me.

It was my senior year of high school, and I had my driver's license. For the first time, I got a small taste of freedom—just a little, but it was mine. Freedom can come in many different forms. For me, it looked like the possibility of being seen.

His name was David, from West Virginia. He was a friend of my brother Charles and often brought his uniform to the dry cleaners where I worked. Each time he walked through the door my heart would race—I didn't know how to name it back then.

I realize now it wasn't just a crush on a man. It was a longing—for gentleness, for respect, for someone to see me as more than an object, more than a burden, more than a girl to control. And to a girl like me—starved for affection, terrified of attention—he felt safe. He wasn't overly charming or forceful. He didn't flirt or push. He simply noticed me, and in that I felt something I hadn't known was missing.

Even now, when I hear the song "Country Roads, Take Me Home," I still think of Dan. Not because of what was, but because of what could have been, had life looked different, had I been different. But sometimes a crush isn't about falling in love. Sometimes it's about remembering what it feels like to be seen with gentleness, even just for a moment.

Some evenings I'd find myself at Charles's house, where our family often gathered. Although my brother Lloyd looked like Elvis, it was Charles who had the voice. He had a way with the guitar that could bring a room to life. We'd all sit in the living room—my parents; Gary and his wife; and Welford and Diane with their partners—singing for hours in harmony.

And David was often there. He didn't say much, didn't try to insert himself, but his presence was steady, kind. He'd sit quietly in the corner, watching, listening, like he understood the fragile beauty of those nights.

Even with my father in the room, those familiar eyes warning me to stay small, I still caught myself glancing David's way. I never dared to speak of what I felt, but I held onto the silent comfort of knowing he was there. Because for a little while, I was surrounded by music, family, and the gentle presence of someone who saw me. And in that, I caught a glimpse of what hope might look like.

I graduated from 71st High School in 1971, but the day came and went without leaving a mark. I don't remember the ceremony, the cap and gown, or even walking across the stage. Those details faded fast, overshadowed by something far more important to me: getting out.

I had made a vow years earlier, and now that time had come to keep it. I was going to turn eighteen that summer, and even though my parents had planned a birthday party, their plans unraveled the moment I told them I was moving out.

Unlike Betty's traumatic escape, mine unfolded more quietly, but that didn't make it less significant. I wasn't running in the middle of the night. I was walking out in broad daylight, determined to choose something different.

✳ · ✳ · ✳

Around that time my parents started going to church—not that it really changed them. But it changed the rhythm of our lives. Sundays became sacred, at least in appearance. We dressed up, showed up, and sat on pews, looking like a family who had it all together.

But the change was only skin deep. The real reason for the shift was an accident—a violent, sobering moment that could have taken my father's life. He had been drinking when he crashed head on into the "Welcome to Fort Bragg" sign. That sign had once stood as a symbol of honor and arrival. For him, it became a barrier. A warning.

He broke his neck in the crash and wore a brace from his neck to his waist for months. It slowed him down, but it didn't soften him. Maybe, for a fleeting moment, the nearness of death got his attention. We kept going to church, week after week. But while others might have seen a man trying to change, I saw something else. The church hadn't transformed him; it had just given him a new place to hide.

It was at that little country church where I met a family—kind, welcoming—people my father surprisingly trusted. They had even invited me into their home a few times. So when I packed my things and made my decision, it was to their house that my father drove me.

The ride over was eerily quiet. No yelling, no threats, no words at all. Just silence. He pulled up, dropped me off, and drove away. And just like that, I was free—or so I thought. Later that night, Betty came and picked me up and took me to live with her. She had always been my protector—fierce, loving, unafraid to stand in the gap when I couldn't. But it didn't take long to realize that even under her roof, I wasn't far enough away. My father still had access to me. The door wasn't fully closed.

So I moved again, this time to stay with Aunt Gussie. She wasn't my warrior like Betty had been, but she was gentle and steady, and her home felt quiet and safe. I needed space to breathe, to sort through what freedom was supposed to feel like.

I started working as a hairdresser at Brandy's Beauty Salon. A few girls who had graduated from cosmetology school with me worked there too. One of them was Pamela. We became fast friends. She introduced me to things I had only imagined—dancing, drinking, nightclubs—and for a while, I felt like I was catching up on the life I never got to live. Eventually, I moved in with Pamela and her mother. It felt like independence. It felt like freedom. But there were shadows I didn't see coming.

There was another woman who worked at the salon—Janice. She was married to a man named Danny Brooks. She was a beautiful woman, tall and slender, with blonde hair that hung straight down her back like a silk curtain. Her beauty was striking, effortless, the kind that drew attention without asking for it.

It was always odd seeing them together. They looked like Mutt and Jeff. She was long and lean, and he was small and wiry. The contrast between them was sharp, almost comical, but there was nothing funny about the stories she shared with us.

Janice used to tell us awful stories about Danny, the way he controlled her, how easily his temper flared, how he demanded everything and gave nothing in return. We listened, but I don't think I truly understood. Not yet.

Danny still came around the salon, bold and unbothered, like none of those stories had ever been spoken aloud. He was a small man, not just in height but in build—always moving with a kind of restless energy.

But what he lacked in size, he made up for in swagger. He carried himself like he was ten feet tall, with the cocky strut of a Bantam rooster, puffed up and full of pride. He drove a sleek, dark luxury sedan, the kind of car that purred like money and power.

To my young, naïve eyes, he seemed exciting, dangerous in a way I couldn't yet name. He had a sharp jawline, piercing eyes and a way of talking that made you feel like you were the only person in the room. He exuded confidence. And to someone like me—inexperienced, eager to be noticed—it felt intoxicating.

One night, Pamela and I went to the Royal Club. Danny was there, not with Janice, but alone. He came over to our table, bought us drinks, and we danced most of the night. It felt lighthearted at first, fun even, the kind of night I had missed out on for so long. But what started as innocent quickly turned into something I wasn't ready for. Before I fully understood what was happening, I found myself in his car driving into the woods. That's where I lost my virginity. Not in love. Not in trust. But in silence, in confusion. In the hands of someone who knew how to take advantage of a girl still learning what it meant to be seen.

The next morning, I went to work with a heart heavy with shame, I knew I'd have to face Janice. She had found blood in the back seat of Danny's car. It was mine. She told us she knew he had been with someone else that night. I said nothing. I couldn't even look at her. I carried the weight of what had happened, though I hadn't yet named it for what it was.

Janice eventually found her way out of that relationship, but I didn't. I had escaped my father's house only to step into another kind of bondage. This one didn't have rules or curfews. It didn't need them—it had a name. It had a grip. And it cast a shadow that would follow me long after the music stopped.

I thought leaving home would fix everything, but I didn't know then that geography doesn't heal wounds, and freedom without wisdom is still a kind of bondage.

I had run from my father's house into a world I wasn't prepared for. I thought I could taste adulthood, but I didn't yet understand its cost. I made decisions not out of confidence, but out of emptiness. Out of a strong desire to be wanted, to be loved, to be seen. But the truth is, when you chase freedom without healing, you often run headfirst into new chains.

Wisdom from Galatians 6:7 says, *"Do not be deceived: God is not mocked, for whatever one sows that will he also reap"* (ESV). I had sown in pain, I had sown without understanding, and now I was reaping confusion, shame, and a prison with no bars—walls I couldn't yet climb.

Yet even in there, even in the consequence of my choices, God was present. He didn't shame me; He didn't abandon me. He met me in the wreckage.

That's the beauty of grace. We can't always undo what we've done, but God can redeem it. And even our detours, our mistakes, our broken places become part of the path He uses to bring us home.

Chapter 9

From the Frying Pan into the Fire

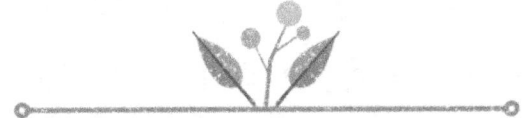

WHEN DANNY AND JANICE SEPARATED, I moved in with him—never realizing I was trading one captor for another. By the time the truth set in, the door had already locked behind me. From the outside, it looked like a dream—a large brick home that was brand new and far bigger than the one I grew up in. But beauty can be deceiving.

Inside, the silence echoed. The emptiness pressed in from every wall. It looked like freedom, but it was captivity dressed in finer clothes. Everything Janice had warned me about—the abuse, the control, the darkness—soon became my reality.

She had escaped. I had taken her place.

Danny was White, and he liked to call me his "Indian squaw," as though I were a trophy he had conquered. He carried himself with a mix of charm and control. And I—too broken, too unsure—didn't see it for what it was.

The first night I was with him, in the back seat of his car, I became pregnant. I was eighteen—still a child, without a voice to defend myself. Danny, seven years older and knew exactly what he was doing. He didn't want children, so he made the arrangements. I was told it wasn't really a baby—just a lump of cells. But my heart knew otherwise. Something inside me broke.

Sadly, it happened again. Both times, the same arrangements. The same silence. The same grief. I still wonder—were they boys? Girls? What would they have been like if I had been stronger? I carry them in my heart, believing that when I leave this world, I will see them, and they will know me.

We lived just outside Fayetteville. By then, I had already pulled away from my family—maybe to avoid rejection before it came. Danny made me quit my job, cutting away the last thread of independence I had. He controlled everything.

When he went out at night—to strip clubs and bars—he removed the phone speaker so I couldn't make calls. He pulled the coil wires from my car so I couldn't drive. Even if I wanted to leave, there was nowhere to go.

Danny didn't want a homemaker; he wanted a showpiece. When he came home from work, I was expected to look as if I had stepped off a fashion runway. He spared no expense—boutique outfits styled from head to toe, matching shoes, handbags, jewelry, lipstick. I had long black hair and hazel eyes that caught the light when I wore makeup. But the woman in the mirror felt like a stranger. It was a Cinderella story with a Beauty and the Beast ending—glass slippers and polished carriages under the rule of a man who wanted possession, not love.

The only light in that dark place came when he was away at work. That's when I met my neighbors—Kara next door, Lila across the street, and Susan, Lila's sister. Together, we laughed. We cried. We survived.

My house became our gathering place—my refuge. For a few precious hours, I could breathe, be myself, and remember that I was human. Danny didn't mind, as long as they were gone before he came home and as long as they stayed within the boundaries he set. It wasn't freedom, but it was enough to keep going.

In my naïveté, I thought I had escaped one prison, but I had stepped into another—this one wrapped in expensive clothes, polished shoes, and quiet control. The chains were harder to see, but just as heavy to carry.

Even there, in the darkest corners of that house, God was present. I couldn't always feel Him. I couldn't always hear Him. But He saw me.

"Even the darkness is not dark to You; the night is bright as the day, for darkness is as light with You."

—Psalm 139:12 (ESV)

Sometimes we mistake rescue for love. Sometimes we mistake survival for freedom. True freedom begins when we stop running from the past and start trusting the One who can redeem it. And even there, He was already leading me out.

Chapter 10

Life in the Fast Lane

I WAS SETTLING INTO MY NEW, lavish lifestyle—the best of everything at my fingertips. For the first time in my life, I could create a home of my own, and I poured myself into it. From the wallpaper to the carpet, the furniture to the custom drapes—I chose it all.

It wasn't just a house; it was a statement. A stage. My sanctuary and my showplace. Red became my signature—bold, fierce, alive. Velvet throws and silk pillows. Roses in every room.

The dining room shimmered in red and gold, the walls brushed with a metallic sheen that caught the light just right. Ornate lamps, mirrored accents, high-backed chairs—my living room felt like a throne room.

I felt like Scarlett O'Hara in lace and silk. And Danny—my Rhett Butler—lavished me with everything I could ever want... except what I needed most. Because no matter how beautiful the house looked, it was still a prison.

The party life was cinematic. I drove a deep emerald-green Jaguar that glimmered like a jewel in the sun. My long black hair streamed behind me like a ribbon of silk. Designer dresses hugged my curves, each one a piece of art. When we entered a club, heads turned.

Conversations stopped. We were the power couple—him with swagger, me on his arm like a prize.

We danced. We drank. We did drugs and smoked pot. We partied until dawn under lights brighter than my own joy. But behind every toast, every photograph, every perfect smile, a voice inside me was begging—to be more than beautiful, to be real.

Sometimes I visited my family—stepping out of the Jaguar in heels that clicked against the pavement, sunglasses on, hair cascading like a magazine cover. To them, I must have looked like a star. Gary would laugh and call me "Miss High Hat," poking fun at the glamour I wore like armor.

Betty wasn't fooled. She saw through the car, the clothes, the curated smiles. She kept her distance, spoke her truth, and Danny hated her for it—because she couldn't be bought.

The rest of my siblings? They adored him. Gifts, charm, generosity—he could buy loyalty with a flash of his wallet, and he did.

But not Betty. And that made her dangerous to him.

One year, I took Gary and his family to Disney World—all expenses paid. Their faces lit up as we stepped onto Main Street, U.S.A.—wide-eyed, taking it all in. We rode rides, chased characters, ate too much popcorn, and ended the night under fireworks bursting like magic across the sky. For a moment, I wasn't just a trophy. I was the one giving joy.

✳ · ✳ · ✳

Then came the day that split my world in two. It was 1974. I was going about my day when I heard it on the radio—a young woman killed in a car accident at a gas station. Something in me froze. Minutes later, the phone rang. Betty's voice broke: "Diane is dead."

Time stopped. My wild, beautiful, broken sister—gone. The accident wasn't just a headline. It was my blood. A part of me shattered.

At the funeral home, Betty and I did her hair and makeup—the last act of love we could give. She had dyed her hair dark the night before. It didn't look like her. My bold, blonde sister—lifeless, unfamiliar.

After the funeral, we gathered at my parents' house. The air was thick with grief, alcohol, and years of unspoken pain. And then Danny, with that mocking glint in his eye, lowered himself into my father's lap like it was a joke—daring him to react. My father swung. Danny ducked. The blow landed across my face. I staggered back, stunned— not just from the hit, but from the moment itself.

Mourning my sister, barely holding it together, and now this— from the man who never knew how to protect me. It wasn't the last time I saw my father, but it was the last time his anger ever left its mark on me.

Months later, Betty called again. "Please, go see Daddy. He's in the hospital. It's bad." I said no at first. Too much pain. Too much history. But something in me—maybe guilt, maybe grace—softened. And I went.

He lay in the bed, tubes in his arms, monitors blinking. Our eyes met for a moment before the alarms screamed. Doctors rushed in. I was ushered into the hallway. They moved him to Chapel Hill for emergency surgery.

The surgery was a success—until his body rejected the heart meant to save him. He died on the operating table.

The funeral was packed—friends, neighbors, customers from his barbershop. People stood and told stories about the man they loved. I sat in silence. Dry-eyed. While the world mourned their hero, I mourned nothing. I wasn't grieving the man in the casket. I was grieving the life he stole from me—the innocence, the safety, the voice I buried just to survive.

And while one life was being buried, another was growing inside me. Two months pregnant. No one knew. Not even Danny. This baby was mine. I would protect it with everything I had left.

Two lives gone—Diane and my father. And yet, in the middle of death, there was life.

I didn't know it then, but God was already preparing to break open the shell I had built around my heart. Not with a sudden miracle, but with the slow, steady work of redemption. I had spent years numbing pain, covering wounds with beauty, running from my past. But God doesn't waste anything—not even the ugliest parts of our stories.

"What the enemy meant for harm, God intended for good, to accomplish what is now being done—the saving of many lives."
—Genesis 50:20 (paraphrased)

Chapter 11

The Child He Couldn't Refuse

I WAITED. I KNEW THERE WAS A legal window for an abortion, and I made sure to wait just long enough for that window to close. This time, he wouldn't take this child from me.

When I finally told him, it was over dinner. He was talking about work, his car, his plans for the weekend—everything but me. And then I said it.

"I'm pregnant."

The words hung in the air like smoke. He looked up from his plate, his fork pausing mid-air.

"What?"

His voice was flat at first—like maybe he'd heard me wrong.

"I'm pregnant," I repeated, this time firmer. "And I'm keeping the baby."

He dropped his fork.

"Don't start this again," he snapped. "You know I don't want kids. We've been through this before."

"We have," I said. "And this time, I made the decision before you had a say."

He stood up, pacing.

"You can still take care of it," he snapped. "It's not too late."

"Yes, it is," I said calmly, holding his gaze. "I waited. I know the law. That window is closed—and I'm not going through that again."

He clenched his jaw, his hands balled into fists at his sides. The heat in his eyes wasn't just anger—it was fear, maybe even pain, but it came out as rage. He stopped mid-step and stared at me.

"You planned this," he said through gritted teeth. "You waited on purpose."

Silence stretched between us. He ran his hand through his hair and let out a heavy, bitter sigh. I could see the anger still burning behind his eyes, but also something else—resignation. He didn't nod. He didn't speak. He just sat down and lit a cigar, like a man who knew he'd lost the fight.

And that was it.

He never said he was okay with it—but he didn't fight me again. Not because he understood. Not because he changed. But because *this time*, he didn't have a choice.

"I did," I replied, without apology. "Because this time, you don't get to decide. This baby is mine."

I understand now where that anger and rage came from. Like my siblings Lloyd, Diane, and Welford, Danny had been given away as a child. Sent to live with his aunt and uncle because his parents couldn't afford to raise all their children. There was no scandal or infidelity, just poverty—too many mouths, and too little means. But no child understands that. And maybe that's why he never wanted children—because he had been one that no one fought to keep.

I was almost six months pregnant when the wedding plans—if you could call them that—finally came together. We drove down to Dillon, South Carolina, known for quick ceremonies and quiet paperwork. There was no bouquet, no lace, no dream dress—just a rushed arrangement to make things look "respectable."

My brother Charles, along with Gary and Welford, came to support me. Their presence meant something—familiar faces in a moment that didn't feel like mine.

Betty wasn't there. Whether she refused to come or I wasn't allowed to invite her, I'm not sure. But her absence stung. We joked about it being a shotgun wedding, as if laughing could dull the reality. But everyone knew the truth. This wasn't love. This was damage control.

There I stood—this little Indian princess, barely twenty-two, with a round belly pressing against a borrowed dress, marrying a man who never wanted to be a husband or a father. But he had no choice. And somehow, that made me feel stronger—not because I had won, but because I had survived.

I walked into that chapel not as a blushing bride, but as a girl who had already been through too much—standing at the altar to claim what little dignity she could.

As the weeks passed, I busied myself preparing for the arrival of my baby. Danny had gone out of town for work leaving me to gather everything on my own. The crib, the baby clothes, the blankets—it was all up to me. But I didn't mind. I was happy to do it. This baby was mine—a life I had fought to protect, and I was preparing to welcome him into the world.

It was New Year's Eve, 1974, when the first pains began. I don't even remember who took me to the hospital. Maybe a neighbor.

Maybe Kara. Everything was a blur. All I remember is that I was alone. Danny was out of town working—as always.

While the rest of the world was celebrating and counting down to midnight, I was counting contractions—my body aching and trembling as labor took over. But it wasn't quick. Forty-eight hours of grueling, relentless labor. Pain so intense it felt like it would split me into two.

And then finally—in January 1975—my baby boy arrived.

But when they placed that tiny body in my arms, everything I had dreamed of was wrapped in warm skin and soft cries. I had never seen anything more beautiful. His head looked like a football—long and pointed from the long, hard labor. Everyone joked, and he quickly earned the nickname "Football Head." But after a few days, it rounded out just fine.

He had dark brown hair, soft and full, and piercing brown eyes that seemed far too wise for a newborn. His skin was flawless—the perfect blend of my Indian heritage and his White father's world.

He was strong. He was stunning. He was mine.

We were already back home and settled in before Danny finally returned—two weeks later—to meet his son. And of course, he had to be named after his father. It wasn't up for discussion—it was a demand. So we called him Little D.

And just like that, the man who didn't want children was suddenly smitten. From the moment he laid eyes on that baby, something shifted. The little Bantam rooster of a man puffed up with pride, strutting like the world needed to know he'd done something worth celebrating.

"That's my boy," he said to anyone who would listen. Danny Brooks's son. His pride and joy.

He couldn't stop looking at him. Couldn't stop talking about him. And from the first moment, he decided he would spoil him rotten— nothing was too good for his son. For all his flaws, for all his fire, I truly believe that was the first time Danny understood what love looked like—not the kind he had received, but the kind he was finally able to give.

And though Danny would never say it out loud, I could see something shifting behind his eyes—a softening. He had been given away as a child. Now here he was—a father—and this time, he was the one doing the claiming.

This child bore his name. This child was his. It didn't erase the damage, but it revealed something deeper. Maybe, just maybe, love had found a way to reach the boy who was once left behind.

There are moments in life when we stand at a crossroads—when life and death, blessing and curse are set before us. And though fear whispered one thing, faith answered louder.

"This day I call the heavens and the earth as witnesses against you that I have set before you life and death, blessings and curses. Now choose life, so that you and your children may live."
—Deuteronomy 30:19

This time, I chose life. Not because it was easy. Not because I had all the answers. But because deep in my spirit, I knew—God was asking me to trust Him with what I could not yet see.

Danny didn't want a child. He had already taken that choice from me not once but twice. But this time, the choice was mine.

And I made it.

That day, I chose life. And in doing so, I chose love. I chose hope. I chose to break the cycle. My son wasn't just a second chance. He was the beginning of redemption.

Chapter 12

Running on Empty

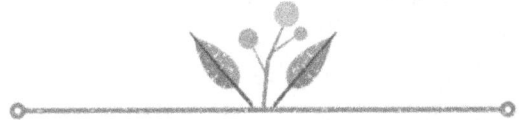

NO ONE TOLD ME WHAT THE life of a mother with a newborn really looked like. No one told me about the kind of tired that settles into your bones, or the loneliness that creeps in—even with a baby in your arms. I need you to see me. Not the polished version. Not the one people waved to in the grocery store. I need you to see the real me—sitting in the dim light of the nursery, hair matted from sleepless nights, milk-stained clothes clinging to a body I barely recognized, rocking back and forth while tears slid silently down my face. I wasn't crying because I didn't love my baby. I was crying because I was exhausted, overwhelmed, and silently drowning in something I didn't yet have a name for: postpartum depression.

But thank God for Kara, my next-door neighbor. She was always there when I needed her—showing up like a quiet angel with a soft voice and helping hands. Her little girl Shelby, just six years old, would watch me breastfeed and in her innocent honesty, started calling me "chocolate momma." I guess it was the dark color of my skin—and as strange as it sounds, it made me laugh when nothing else could.

And then there was Danny's Aunt Maime. Petite, with soft silver hair curled perfectly in place—she seemed to step out of another era, grace still clinging to her. There was a sweetness about her, a warmth that made you feel safe—but underneath it, a strength you didn't dare challenge. You didn't get anything past Maime. She saw through excuses, but never judged—she just loved.

She adored Little D. He wasn't just her great-nephew—he was her grandchild. Her heart. She'd bundle him in a blanket and take him for drives until he fell asleep. She brought toys, rocked him to sleep, whispered sweet nothings, and beamed with pride every time she held him. He was precious to her—sweet and spoiled in the best kind of way. And in the moments when I was worn thin and couldn't give anymore, Maime showed up—pot in hand, apron on, filling the kitchen with the smells of something warm and good. She fed our bellies and our spirits, one quiet act of love at a time. She filled in the gaps with love and steady presence—never asking for anything in return.

Danny traveled often, gone for weeks at a time. And when he came home, it wasn't with tenderness or care—it was with expectation. He still wanted the carefree girl he had met—the one with perfect makeup, hair done, ready to drink and dance all night. But I wasn't that girl anymore. I was a mother—tired, breastfeeding, sleep-deprived, and still aching from childbirth. Sometimes I tried to go with him on his trips, but traveling with a baby was nearly impossible. So most of the time, it was just me and Little D., home alone.

One day, Danny looked at me—a young woman at twenty-two who once turned every head in the room.

"You're old, fat, and ugly," he told me.

Those words cut through me like glass. He used to call me his Indian princess. Now, I wasn't even a trophy wife. I was just the mother of his son. And in his eyes, that made me less.

"You're nothing without me," he said. "You'll never be anything without me."

Those words haunted me for years.

He loved Little D.—no doubt about that. He spoiled him, showed him off, treated him like a prize. But while I was home—exhausted, breastfeeding, doing everything to raise his son—he was spending time at Rudy's Lounge, taking what he wanted.

She was the waitress there—tall, blonde, beautiful—a mirror of his first wife. His next obsession. His next conquest. He didn't pursue women to love them. He pursued them to possess them. And while he paraded her around, I was left behind. Discarded. Unseen. Replaced.

What's done in the dark always finds its way to the light—and Danny's affair was no exception. He thought he could sneak, lie, and hide behind the smoky lights of the lounge. But secrets always slip through cracks. The truth clawed its way to the surface. His obsession with the waitress couldn't stay hidden forever. And I was done pretending not to see.

One night, I arranged for a babysitter then slid behind the wheel of my station wagon and headed downtown—straight to Haywood Street, where the strip clubs lit up the night, and Rudy's Lounge sat in the center like a neon crown. I parked across the street and waited, watching the neon flicker like a fuse burning down. When the lights dimmed and the bar emptied, there he was—Danny, strutting like a Bantam rooster, chest puffed, ego blazing, with that waitress on his arm and her friend trailing behind.

He walked to his bright red sports car—his pride, his trophy on wheels. The waitress slid in tight beside him. She looked proud to be chosen. He looked smug. I looked on—burning.

The next moment can only be described as temporary insanity— white-hot rage driving every move. As soon as he pulled out, I followed. Not slowly. Not cautiously. The station wagon might've been a mom car, but that night, it was a missile. As soon as he saw me in his rearview, he hit the gas. The chase was on.

He pulled over. Maybe he thought I'd stop—but I didn't.

I rammed the front of my station wagon into his sports car—a clean, deliberate hit. Steel met steel. The sound of impact became the voice I hadn't been allowed to use. He pulled away—fast. The sports car roared through downtown Fayetteville like a scene from a movie. I followed, relentlessly.

Then—sirens. Red and blue flashing in my rearview. But I wasn't running from them. I was hunting him. I didn't want to be heard. I needed to be seen.

Up Haywood Hill we flew—fast, furious, unstoppable. At the top, he stopped. But rage has no brakes. I hit him again—hard. My station wagon folded in. His sports car—with a steel bar across the back—held up. The next thing I knew, the police had me on the ground, cuffing my wrists behind me.

"That's my wife!" Danny shouted.

The police hesitated. I used that moment. I lunged at the car, grabbed her by the hair, and dragged her out. She clawed, screamed, but I didn't let go—until the police dragged me away and shoved me into the back of the patrol car like I was the criminal in the story I'd been trying to survive.

The door slammed. The world went quiet. That backseat felt like a cage. I sat there—breath heaving, wrists burning. Outside: voices, flashing lights, judgment. Inside: silence.

Danny didn't have his license, so she drove him away in his sports car. The woman I had just dragged from the car was now driving him home. She didn't look back. Neither did he. And me? I sat caged, seething, watching the taillights of my humiliation fade into the night.

A tow truck hauled my station wagon away—crushed, totaled. Just like me. At the station, they didn't book me. No cell. No mugshot. Just a quiet warning—"You should contact an attorney."

But the weight I felt wasn't legal. It was maternal. What about my baby? Where was Little D.? What if I hadn't come home? I called Kara. She came without question—like always.

When I got home, Danny was lying on the floor beside our son's crib. Silent. Still. He didn't speak. Didn't look at me. Just laid there like nothing had happened. And me? I was too tired to scream. Too numb to cry. I walked past him and went to bed. Not a word spoken.

But everything had changed. That night, something shifted. The rage didn't end in glass and gravel. It whispered, *It's time to get out.* And that whisper became my plan for escape. Betrayal stings deeper than anger. That night, I wasn't just chasing a man—I was chasing everything I had lost: Trust. Identity. Dignity.

And in the aftermath, when the rage cooled, all I felt was the ache. The ache of knowing I had stepped outside who I was. That my storm had come from a deeper wound. I was a mother. A woman. A broken girl trying to survive. But my baby slept while I spiraled. My body drove the car. But it was my pain that held the wheel.

"Be sure your sin will find you out." —Numbers 32:23 (ESV)

Not just Danny's sin, but mine too. Because when we trade truth for vengeance, when we lash out instead of laying it down before God, we lose more than control—we lose pieces of our soul. But even in that dark place, God didn't turn away. He didn't abandon me. He let me break so I could begin to heal.

Chapter 13

Cracks in the Mirror

T HE NIGHT BEFORE HAD ENDED in a standoff—rage, fear, could have even resulted in death—but in the morning, there was not even a mention of it. No apology. No remorse—just silence.

Last night, he lay there on the floor next to our baby, like a man keeping watch—not over me, but over his claim. That was the moment I understood. He didn't care about me. He didn't even care about the waitress. He would protect that child—his child—no matter what.

And I—I had to get out. I had to find a way, even if it meant risking everything.

A few days later, he gave me a new car—a burgundy station wagon. Long and sleek, nothing like my old station wagon. It was the kind of car a family woman might drive, but it still had flash—chrome trim, burgundy paint that shimmered like wine in the sun, leather seats that stuck to the back of your legs in the heat. It was nice. I couldn't deny that. He knew I loved red—every shade of it.

Maybe that car was his apology. Not with words, of course—he never had those. But with things. Expensive things. Shiny things. That car was his way of saying, stay. His way of pacifying the fire he had no intention of putting out.

And a part of me—the tired part—wanted to believe it meant something. But deep down, I knew: it wasn't a gift. It was a leash. A long one, maybe, but a leash just the same.

While I got the station wagon, he had his sports car restored— dark, glossy, and sharp enough to catch every eye on the road. It wasn't just a paint job. It was artwork. That car was his pride. His ego, polished to perfection. Sleek. Fast. Untouchable.

It got the royal treatment, pampered like a trophy. I got the illusion of freedom.

He no longer trusted me to stay home. Not after the way I'd snapped. So from that point on, I was to travel with him—with my baby, Little D., in tow. Different cities. Different states. He never stayed in one place too long. Always chasing work, deals, and the next high.

At home, he was flashy and expensive—fast cars, designer clothes, cash flowing like water. But on the road, he was cheap. We weren't living it up in luxury hotels. We stayed in weekly-rate motels—the kind where everything felt temporary and tired. A stained coffee pot. A rusty hotplate, if we were lucky. Cigarette burns on the comforter. Paper-thin walls and that sour motel smell that clung to your clothes and spirit.

While he worked, I was trapped. Pacing worn carpet with a growing baby and nowhere to go. No car. No friends. Just the sound of trucks on the highway and the silence pressing in.

Eventually, I started complaining. The walls were closing in. Silence felt too loud. I was losing myself in those rooms—just a mother, rocking a baby, nowhere to go. And my complaints didn't help. They only made things worse.

I think he got tired of having us around. A woman and a baby didn't fit the life he was chasing. Even in strange cities, there was always a party. Always someone to impress. We were in the way. Little D.—innocent as he was—was a reminder of a responsibility he didn't really want.

My son was growing into a toddler. He was learning to walk, to talk, to laugh—and I was watching it all happen from the edge of a motel bed. There were moments of joy, sure, but fear was always close behind. Fear of what he was growing up in. And fear that I wouldn't get us out.

Eventually, he stopped taking us on trips. Maybe he thought I'd settled down. Maybe he just wanted more freedom. Either way, Little D. and I stayed home.

It felt like peace. But it was only a quieter prison.

After I stopped breastfeeding, I started smoking marijuana again. Just to take the edge off. To feel calm. But one thing led to another. Danny started dealing to support our habits. It started with marijuana. Then came cocaine. The parties got louder. The nights got longer. The money came fast. And we were drowning in it—without even realizing we were sinking.

Even in all the noise, I never let go of the idea of escape. It lived inside me like a heartbeat—steady and waiting. I never said it out loud. Not to anyone but Kara. Kara was more than a neighbor—she was my lifeline. She saw the girl still holding onto hope. The one still trying to find a way out. When I said, "I can't do this anymore," she didn't ask questions. She said, "Let's figure it out."

She had an aunt in New Jersey. Far enough to start over. Quiet enough to disappear. It wasn't a perfect plan, but it was more than I'd had in years. We made arrangements in secret. Quiet phone calls. Whispers across the fence. She told me what to pack. What not to say.

How to time it just right. All I had to do was wait for the night—and be brave enough to go.

That night came. Danny was out partying. I didn't know when he'd be back. I didn't care. I moved through the house like a ghost, hands trembling as I packed. A few clothes. Diapers. Bottles. A blanket. No photos. No keepsakes. Nothing that could slow me down. I took $10,000 from our stash—drug money we never counted. I didn't feel guilty. Not for a second.

I carried my baby to the burgundy station wagon. That night, it wasn't a gift. It was a getaway car. I strapped him in, started the engine, and looked one last time at the house I thought I'd never escape. Then I drove. We left in the middle of the night. I didn't know what would happen in New Jersey. I just knew I wasn't going to let my son grow up in that madness.

We pulled into Kara's aunt's driveway running on fumes. I didn't know the people. Or what would come next. But we were safe. Kara's aunt welcomed us. A warm bed. Kind eyes. A quiet space. For the first time in years, I slept without fear. I watched my son giggle in the sunlight. It was peaceful.

But it didn't last—Danny found us. He threatened Kara—and under pressure, she broke. She told him where I was. I don't blame her. We were all afraid.

I'll never forget the sound of that sports car pulling into the driveway. That engine wasn't just loud—it was a warning. He made it clear—at gunpoint—I was going back. And before dragging us back, he called it a "fresh start."

He wanted to take us to New York City. Show us a good time. No plan. No destination. Just us—crammed into the front seat. Pretending. For one breath, it felt real. But it wasn't. It never was.

Eventually, we drove upstate. Winding roads. Mountain trees. Quiet. He laughed. Took pictures. Acted like we were just another couple on a weekend getaway. Then we returned to pick up my station wagon. I followed his sports car.

But this time, I wasn't chasing anything. I was just following. He led. I followed. And with every mile, I felt the control tightening around my throat. We pulled into the driveway. I didn't move. Before I could unbuckle my seatbelt, he appeared at my window.

"I will kill you if you ever try to leave me again," he said low and matter-of-fact. No shouting. No drama. Just a promise—as if it were already decided. As if he owned the ending.

I looked at my son—still so small. Still so full of light. And I knew. He was never the threat. He was the possession. I wasn't just trying to stay alive. I was trying to keep myself alive. Because Danny didn't see a mother and child. He saw what belonged to him. And men like that don't let go. Not without a fight. Not without blood.

There were still battles ahead. More pain. More lessons. But something inside me had shifted. I knew the truth: I was not his. I was God's. And even in that darkness, even in that prison of fear and control, I clung to this hope:

"The Lord is close to the brokenhearted and saves those who are crushed in spirit." —Psalm 34:18

I was broken. I was crushed. But I was not alone. Not then. Not ever.

Chapter 14

Dancing with the Devil

I STAYED IN THE DRIVER'S SEAT, staring at the side door that led from the garage into the house. My hands were frozen on the steering wheel, my heart strangely quiet—not pounding, not racing, just still. Numb.

Through the open passenger-side window, Danny leaned in, unbuckled our little boy, and lifted him into his arms without a word. He didn't look at me. He didn't need to.

But at that moment, my son's face glowed with joy. His dark brown curls bounced as he wrapped his tiny arms around Danny's neck. His skin, sun-kissed and flawless, made his chubby cheeks lift into a grin. His eyes sparkled with a peace I couldn't name—a peace I had never known. To him, this was home. The only one he'd known. What his little heart understood of mommy and daddy still felt safe. Still felt whole. He giggled softly, resting his head on his father's shoulder, perfectly content. He didn't see the prison I was walking back into—he just saw love.

They disappeared through the side door, leaving me outside with his words still ringing in my ears.

Finally, I opened my door. The creak of it cut the silence like a warning. The air was heavy with the heat of early evening and something darker. I walked slowly toward the side door, each step pulling me further from the pieces of myself I still recognized.

I walked back into that house, but I wasn't the same woman who left it. I had tasted freedom. And once you've tasted freedom, you never forget. You carry it. You dream of it. You fight for it—even in silence. When I stepped inside, his words followed me like a shadow.

The den was the first thing I saw. It wasn't a den anymore—it was the heart of the storm. A large brick fireplace stretched across the far wall, its mantle heavy with dust and forgotten decorations. Above it hung a massive tapestry of dogs playing poker—loud, strange, and out of place, yet somehow perfectly suited to the blurred lines and false bravado of the room.

On the opposite side stood the bar—black leather wrapped sleekly around its frame, more suited to a nightclub than a home. It wasn't just for pouring drinks; it was a symbol of indulgence, secrecy, and control. Beneath it, bottles and baggies were tucked away, ready to fuel nights that bled one into the next.

The furniture was oversized and plush, easy to sink into, easier still to get lost in. The cushions wrapped around you like quicksand disguised in velvet. I surrendered to the lifestyle like someone slipping into warm water—knowing it would drown me, but letting it pull me under anyway.

Danny had built himself a kingdom. He was well known, feared in some circles, respected in others. Judges and attorneys were in his pocket—men who wore robes by day and partied at night. Whether with cash or cocaine, silence was easy to buy, and he bought it often. With them on his side, he didn't just bend the law—he broke it, buried it, and dared anyone to dig it up. That made him untouchable. And me? Invisible.

Keeping up with the party lifestyle came at a cost, and the one who paid it was my son. While the nights blurred into laughter, drugs, and deals, he was passed from hand to hand. The teenage girls in the neighborhood—barely older than children themselves—became his caregivers. They fed him, played with him, bathed him. Somehow, they filled the gap with love. Over time, they became like family.

Judy Blake—my sweet little Judy—lived just down the street. Her mama was Lumbee like me, her daddy White. She was the oldest of three, a tiny blonde-haired girl with big curls and hand-me-down clothes that never quite fit. Quiet, tender-hearted, full of light—she became like my own daughter. She showed up at my door in the early mornings, never knocking, ready to play with my boy while I sat in the den with coffee in one hand and a joint in the other, trying to push away the fog from the night before. Judy never asked questions. She just brought love.

Then there was Darlene—Dar. Taller, louder, full of energy. She would fling open the door and yell, "Mama!" like she was stepping onstage. She brought life with her—bold, colorful, unapologetic. Where Judy was gentle, Dar was wild. Both loved my son, and he loved them.

Maime and HB—Danny's aunt and uncle—were more like grandparents to our boy. Maime, graceful and dignified, carried a quiet strength. HB, jolly and playful, brought joy wherever he went. They cared for my son with steady, unconditional love, often keeping him for days. They never spoke of what they knew about our home, but their presence gave him something stable, something safe.

There were rare moments when it was just my son and me. We'd walk down to the lake, crossing the old railroad tracks. He loved balancing along the wooden planks, arms stretched wide, laughing as he wobbled. Years later, he would tell me those were some of his best memories. He remembered picnics by the bridge, two miles away, and the day I held his hand across the high trussell, teaching him to conquer his fears. He saw strength in me I didn't know I had.

Those walks were small mercies—brief pockets of peace where I could simply be his mother. But the walk always ended. As we neared home, the thump of music would rise from inside, the smell of smoke and stale liquor greeted us at the door. In moments, the peace was gone, replaced by the blur of the life I was living.

Danny's kingdom was guarded—not just by people, but by Valen, a massive attack-trained Doberman. He was a living symbol of fear, pacing in his chain-link enclosure, ready to strike at Danny's command. Sometimes he disappeared for weeks. I didn't ask questions. I preferred the quiet.

Eventually, I learned the truth. During those disappearances, Valen had been staying with another woman—the waitress. The same one I had once dragged out of Danny's sports car. She wasn't just a fling; she was part of his second life. Another home. Another version of him, hidden just outside of town.

How I found out... that's a story I'll never forget.

Looking back, I realize I was living in the middle of a storm I helped create but didn't know how to escape. I had surrendered—not just to a man or a lifestyle—but to fear and survival. Yet even then, God didn't leave me alone.

Kara, my dearest friend, had faded from my daily life under Danny's control. But God sent others—Judy, Dar, Maime, and HB— people who showed up when I couldn't show up for myself. They cared for my son in ways I couldn't. They were grace in human form.

And even in the darkest valley, God was there.

"Even though I walk through the valley of the shadow of death, I will fear no evil, for You are with me." —Psalm 23:4 (ESV)

I had no words for Him then, but He never left. His mercy came in small ways—through people, through protection, through the strength to take the next breath. The valley was never empty.

Chapter 15

Under Surveillance

D ARLENE, MY LOUD AND LOYAL babysitter—my ride-or-die—was with me that fateful day. A flamboyant tomboy, she was always ready for adventure. Mature beyond her years, Dar liked to know everything—where we were going, what we were doing, and when we'd be back. She was the organizer. But when things veered off course, she didn't panic—she adapted. So when I whipped the car around in the middle of the road, tires screeching, she didn't scream. She just sat up straighter and said, "Alright, Mama, what's the pl..."

What started as a simple trip to the grocery store changed in an instant. We had just pulled onto the main street when I saw her—the waitress. The other woman. She was driving her little blue Honda like she owned the road—and my life. Our eyes locked for one sharp second. Recognition. Then, without hesitation, she stuck her hand out the window and flipped me off.

That was all I needed.

I gripped the wheel of my old station wagon—definitely not built for sharp turns—and spun it around. The tires howled, but I didn't care. I was chasing her down. Broad daylight. Right down Main Street. We flew past the lake, through the heart of town, not slowing for anything.

She knew where she was going. At the edge of town, she veered left onto a narrow dirt road. I nearly missed it.

"There! Turn left, Mama!" Dar shouted, pointing through the windshield.

Dust exploded around us as we bounced down the path. Her blue Honda had already pulled into a gravel driveway. She was trying to lose us. But Dar was locked in.

We watched her sprint into a rundown single-wide trailer at the end of the lot. Gravel crunched under our tires as we pulled up behind her. The front door swung open.

To my surprise, she stepped out—with Danny's dog, Valen, on a leash, headed straight for my car.

Dar gasped. "Oh my God, Mama—it's Valen. Be careful! That dog's dangerous!"

She was right. Valen was trained to attack. He wasn't my dog. He was Danny's. A weapon.

But adrenaline had taken over. I stepped out, not even closing the door behind me.

Valen hesitated. He looked confused. His ears perked. His muscles tightened. He had lived in my home. Knew my voice. My scent. He was caught between us.

She barked the command: "Valen—attack!"

My heart dropped.

I shouted, "Valen, stay!"

Two voices. Two commands. One choice.

He froze—body taut, eyes flicking between us. He didn't know who to obey.

"Get back in the car, Mama!" Dar yelled, her voice cracking. "Please! Don't trust that dog!"

I didn't move. We stood there—me, the waitress, and Danny's dog—locked in a moment that could've ended in tragedy. But somehow—by instinct or grace—I turned and climbed back in.

As I pulled the door closed, she lunged forward and slammed it behind me. In her fury, she caught her own hand in the frame. Later, I heard she broke two fingers. One of them? The middle one she used on me earlier. That was poetic justice.

I'd learned not to confront Danny about his affairs. There was no truth to gain. No peace to win. So life continued. But something inside me turned cold. Knowing he had another life—one outside our walls—ignited something in me. Rage. A hunger to retaliate. So I sought her out.

I asked questions. Dug around. And found out she worked during the day at the drug store at the mall. I didn't plan to forgive. I planned revenge.

Dar was with me again. My partner in petty crime. A bag of sugar sat beside us in the car.

We found her Honda in the lot. I pulled up, opened her gas tank, and dumped the sugar in—no hesitation. Later, I heard the engine was ruined. It was reckless. And it felt good.

But after the rush wore off... something else settled in. This life I was living—this woman I was becoming—felt foreign. What began as survival was becoming retaliation. Control. Pride.

❋ · ❋ · ❋

Then came the disco years. If I couldn't feel peace, I'd settle for distraction. The dance club sat high above the city with spinning lights and pounding music. The movie *Staying Alive* hit the screens—and that became my mantra: Just stay alive!

I danced through the pain. Escaped into the music. Forgot through the drugs. I stopped caring where Danny was—or who he was with. My anger had burned out. I was numb.

That's when I became close to Lillian. She was the life of the party—bold, wild, electric. Everyone knew her. Her confidence was magnetic. When Danny was out of town, we found the fun—and the men. That's how I met Sam.

Handsome. Smooth. Dangerous in a quiet way. At first, it was innocent. Drinks. Music. Games. But then came the affair.

Sam made me feel seen—desired—worth something. And I gave in—not because I didn't know better, but because I didn't know any different.

We played backgammon. And while we sat around that table, I was playing chess with my life. Because Danny had eyes everywhere—the babysitters, neighbors, "friends" who reported back.

It didn't take long. He flew home. He didn't come in shouting. He came in hunting. He found me in the bedroom. No words. He shoved a pillow over my face. I couldn't breathe. This wasn't a threat. It was intent. I thought I would die.

But then—he let go.

I ran—keys in hand. Shaking. Sobbing. I ended up at Lillian's house, collapsing through her door. I don't know why he didn't chase me. But I know this: my life was spared. Lillian let me stay with her. But eventually, the call came.

"It's time to come home."

And like that, I was claimed again—not as a wife, but as a possession. It became clear: revenge had poisoned me. And I wasn't the only one paying the price—my son was watching.

I had brought him into this world. And it was still my job to protect him—even if I hadn't protected myself. He didn't ask to be born into chaos. But none of us do.

Danny and I didn't know how to love because we never saw it modeled. We didn't grow up with tenderness. Or safety. But I could choose to give my son something better. Even if I wasn't free yet. Even if I didn't know how.

There are seasons where survival doesn't look brave—it just looks like not giving up. I wasn't strong because I had it all together. I was strong because I kept going. One breath at a time.

God's hand was still on me—even when I didn't know how to reach back. And now, when I look back, one scripture rises from the rubble:

"The light shines in the darkness, and the darkness has not overcome it." —John 1:5

The darkness tried. But it didn't win.

Chapter 16

A Life Worth Fighting For

T HE DISCO LIGHTS FADED, and with them, the life I had once clung to. Late nights, loud music, glitter and smoke—it all felt like another world. I had surrendered to that life once. It numbed the pain. Helped me forget. But I wasn't that woman anymore. Coming home, I knew something had shifted.

My focus turned to my son. In the midst of chaos, he was my clarity. When I looked at him, laid aside my own pain, something fierce and tender awakened in me—a mother's love. I hadn't seen it modeled. I hadn't been taught. But it was there. And it became my one pure thing. Motherhood grounded me, gave me purpose, and became the thread I held onto when everything else unraveled.

Even Danny seemed different. He slowed down, and spent more time at home. One day, he bought a boat—fire-red, sleek, trimmed in white. Flashy and loud, just like him. It wasn't about the boat. It was about image. Control. Power. But that summer, it also gave us something unexpected: peace.

The lake came alive with the season—kids splashing, motors humming, music floating on the breeze. Families barbecuing, laughter rising like a song. I learned to water ski—falling, crashing, then standing. For the first time in years, I stood. Not just on water—but in spirit.

And I felt free.

On the shoreline, my little boy played in the shallows, curls dripping, joy radiating from him like sunlight. His laughter filled the air. And for that moment, he was simply a child. And I was simply his mother.

Sundays brought dinners with Danny's family. Loud voices, shared meals, cousins racing barefoot through the grass. It reminded me of Aunt Gussie's house—those childhood gatherings rooted in love and noise and food passed hand to hand.

Now I was the one on the porch, watching. Watching my son live a childhood I had only dreamed of. And joy crept in—not loud or flashy. Gentle. Sacred.

Sometimes, the three of us—Danny, our son, and I—walked to the lake together. No tension. No fear. Danny would skip stones and our son would mimic him, eager to please. They'd run down the railroad tracks, laughter echoing through the trees. I watched them and saw a family. Not pretending. Not fractured—whole. Everything I had longed for... was right there.

But summer doesn't last forever. The lake grew quiet. The golden days dimmed. And then it came—my little boy started kindergarten.

And with that, something deep in me mourned. Not just the loss of time, but the innocence we'd never get back. The years that slipped through our fingers while chaos ruled. Letting go hurt in a way I hadn't expected.

On that first day, he clung to my leg in the hallway, his arms wrapped tight. He didn't want to let go. Neither did I.

The classroom was alive with color—tiny chairs, scattered crayons, bookshelves lined with stories waiting to be read. Ms. Jessie greeted us with a calm smile. She was steady, no-frills, and kind. And something in her presence made me feel like he'd be okay.

As her assistant coaxed him away, she turned to me and said, "He'll be just fine. I promise."

I nodded. But I couldn't speak. The tears came fast as I walked out, weeping down the hallway.

Ironically, he adjusted before I did. Within days, he had friends. He was laughing. Exploring. Thriving. It was me who had to catch up. He stepped into a world that no longer revolved around me. And I was left asking—what now?

Kara had moved. The nightlife no longer called my name. What made me happiest was picking him up each day, seeing his joy, hearing his stories. Most afternoons, I'd have a quick word with Ms. Jessie. Those brief exchanges turned into longer talks. Before long, she was sitting at my kitchen table, sipping coffee, listening.

And I began to talk. About the past. The pain. The things I had never said aloud. One day, she asked the question that lingered in my soul: "Why did you allow all of that to happen?"

All I could say was, "Because I didn't see a way out."

But she didn't look at me with judgment. She saw something in me I hadn't seen in myself. Jessie once said, "A woman with knowledge is a woman who knows her worth." It wasn't about degrees. It was about dignity. Believing I was capable. That I was enough. And I began to believe her.

She encouraged me to enroll in community college. While my son started school, I did too. I registered without telling Danny. He was away, and for the first time, I didn't ask for permission. I made a decision—for me.

But when he came home, everything changed. He was waiting in the den. Calm. Quiet. A shotgun across his lap. "You will quit school," he said. "I won't allow it."

Fear stirred. But I didn't yield. I stood my ground. Told him no. When he lifted the gun, I lunged. We wrestled. My pinky snapped. Pain tore through me. But I broke free. And I ran. Straight to Lila's, hand throbbing, heart pounding. But I had made it out. I had taken a stand.

And I learned something I would never forget: when you confront a bully, he eventually backs down. And that's exactly what he did.

I stayed in school and my confidence grew. My voice returned. I began to believe my story could change—not just for my son, but for me.

I had learned what it meant to persevere. I didn't ask for the battles, but I faced them. I didn't plan the detours, but I walked through them. I stood my ground. I chose to rise.

"She is clothed with strength and dignity, and she laughs without fear of the future." —Proverbs 31:25 (NLT)

And I was laughing—because I had found a joy I never knew. Motherhood had become my treasure. In all I had lost, I found something worth living for.

Chapter 17

Born into the Storm

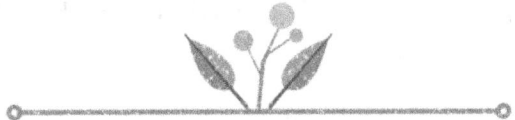

IT BEGAN WITH AN EXHAUSTION I couldn't shake—not just tiredness, but the deep, bone-heavy kind that made getting out of bed feel like a battle. Then came the nausea. I knew—before any test could tell me—I was pregnant again. Unplanned. Unexpected. Life-altering. This wasn't like it had been with my son. It was worse.

Waves of sickness hit from the moment I opened my eyes—sometimes before. I found myself on the bathroom floor, hunched over the toilet, gagging, shaking, trying to breathe through the heaves. Even when there was nothing left in my stomach, my body kept trying to rid itself of something.

The smell of food, the sound of movement, even sunlight made me dizzy. There were days I couldn't keep anything down, and days I didn't have the strength to stand.

This time, the fear wasn't just about the toll on my body. It was about what it would cost me. I had just started building something—school, confidence, purpose. And now, I had to face Danny.

He was oblivious, unless it touched his life directly. But I couldn't avoid telling him. He had just come in from work, a long day in the manholes splicing cable underground. His overalls were stained with dirt and grease, boots tracking mud across the floor. He dropped into a chair, shoulders slumped, sweat clinging to his shirt.

I sat across from him, weary but steady. "I'm pregnant."

He jerked back like I'd struck him, then sprang up, rage flashing. "I don't believe this—not again. I don't want any more children."

I didn't flinch. "Well, you're going to have another child. And that's final."

He stormed from the room, fists clenched, cursing, his rage filling the air like smoke. I stayed still until the storm passed.

I left school the next semester—not because I wanted to, but because I had no strength. Getting my son to school each day was all I could manage.

Life at home with Danny had gotten difficult, so Jessie said Little D. and I could move in with her. She was my steady support, never judging, always encouraging. One afternoon, Jessie told me a story that made us both laugh. "You know," she said, "Little D. writes his full name better than any kid in class. The only problem is, he wrote it perfectly on the bathroom wall." Even in mischief, my boy could make me smile.

As my belly grew, so did my hope. I didn't know the baby's gender, but I prayed for a girl. I pictured my son as a big brother; a home filled with laughter and love.

$$* \cdot * \cdot *$$

It was a sunny Saturday afternoon when a knock came on Danny's door. I was there to pick something up. Little D. was with Maime and HB. Danny was napping. I floated through the quiet house, humming, daydreaming.

The knock came at the side door—the one only people who *belonged* used. I smiled, expecting a neighbor, and opened it.

The waitress from the bar stood there. Even while married to me, Danny had kept his affair with her alive—but it was clear she hadn't expected me to be home. She pushed the screen door open and barged in. "Where's Danny?" she demanded.

"You don't belong here," I told her. But she wasn't listening. She was tall—and fueled by rage. In one motion, she grabbed me—six months pregnant—and threw me across the room. I caught myself, hand to my belly, heart pounding.

She stormed down the hallway toward the bedroom. I followed and saw her rip the covers off the bed, screaming at Danny. He sat up, dazed and guilty. I stood in the doorway shouting for her to leave. Their voices clashed like lightning. I ran to the kitchen and called 911.

"You'd better be gone before the police get here," he finally shouted. She left. Then he left too.

When the police arrived, I told them everything—her name, what she'd done, that I was pregnant. They filed a report and promised a warrant.

Danny never came back to face it.

I called Jessie, and she came without hesitation, taking me to her home. I called Maime and HB to keep Little D. safe for a few days.

When I told Danny I was leaving him for good, he didn't argue. But he said, "You're not taking my son."

The words hit like a blade. How do you walk away with one child inside you, leaving the other behind?

At court, Danny was subpoenaed but didn't show. I stood before the judge, swollen and exhausted. The waitress was charged with assault and ordered to leave the state. That was the last time I saw her.

Danny begged me to come home until the baby was born. I agreed—not for him, but for my son.

He was out of town working when I went to a routine checkup and learned my water had already broken. The hospital was just across the street, so I drove myself, and walked into the ER.

"I'm having a baby."

There was no one beside me—no hand to hold. The nurses were kind, and the labor was short, calm, and peaceful.

She came quickly—like she already knew I needed her. She arrived when I needed something to hold onto. God gave me her—not to replace the love I had for my son, but to add to it. Holding her, I understood what Danny felt when his son was born.

But my love came with a vow: she would not carry the weight of my past. She would not live in fear or silence. I would protect her. I would fight for her. I would teach her to fight for herself.

"Every good and perfect gift is from above, coming down from the Father of lights, who does not change like shifting shadows."
—James 1:17 (CSB)

She was my gift. And I was holding onto it for dear life.

Chapter 18

The Cost of Freedom

T HE MOMENT SHE WAS BORN, everything changed. I had prayed for a little girl, and when they placed her in my arms, I knew I had been given a gift straight from heaven. She was mine, my girl, my angel, my saving grace. The most beautiful little girl I had ever seen. I named her Jatana Lynn.

The name Jatana had lived in my heart long before she was born. It belonged to a neighbor I barely knew, a woman who didn't fit into the party life that surrounded us. But there was something about her, a quiet elegance, a kind of grace I had never seen but always longed for. It wasn't just her name I admired, it was who she was. I decided that if I ever had a daughter, I wouldn't just give her that name, I would raise her to become the kind of woman it represented. I wanted her to have more than I ever did: freedom, identity, strength.

When it came time to pair that name with a middle name, I remembered one of Danny's friends who used to stop by, likely to buy drugs, but her name always struck me: Lynn. It just fit. So Jatana Lynn she became.

When I looked down at her, with that soft blonde hair and those beautiful green eyes, I froze. Wait a minute. This can't be my child. She didn't look like me at all. But I laughed at myself, because deep down

I knew the truth. She was mine. God had given her to me. She filled every broken place inside of me with something I hadn't felt in a long time: hope.

It was more than the birth of a baby. It felt like the birth of a new version of me. Something opened inside of me, something I didn't know was still there. I had spent years surviving, hiding, playing roles just to make it through. But holding her in my arms, I felt like I had been handed a second chance, not just to be a better mother, but to become the woman I had always wanted to be. I saw that hope in her eyes. I saw a life I hadn't dared to imagine. I didn't know how I was going to do it, but I knew I couldn't waste this moment. She was my *why*. Because of her, I started to believe I could finally become the person I was meant to be.

Before she was born, I had made up my mind. I told my OB/GYN that I wanted to have my tubes tied immediately after delivery. I didn't want to risk another pregnancy, not with Danny Brooks. I had tried birth control, even an IUD, but nothing ever seemed to work. The only sure way of taking control of my body and my future was to make it final. No more surprises. No more wondering. No more children with a man who had brought me nothing but pain.

This decision wasn't just medical. It was emotional, spiritual, and deeply personal. I was drawing a line in the sand. I wasn't just done having children. I was done with him. I didn't want a future that included Danny Brooks in any part of it. I had spent enough years surviving his chaos, walking on eggshells, losing pieces of myself. That part of my life was over. My life was moving forward, and it would do so without him.

Little by little, the Lord was binding up my broken heart and releasing me from the chains that had held me captive for so long. I was starting to see the light of freedom dawning on the horizon.

"He has sent me to bind up the brokenhearted, to proclaim freedom for the captives and release from darkness for the prisoners." —Isaiah 61:1

Chapter 19

Living What I Learned

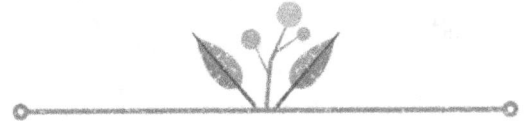

W HAT HAPPENED TO THE GIRL behind the chair in the corner of the living room, with its faded plaid seat, sunken cushion, and faint smell of old smoke woven into its fabric? That chair wasn't just furniture. It was her hiding place. Her shield.

She grew up. She didn't vanish. She learned to function. She built walls made of strength, silence, and smiles that said, "I'm fine."

But behind those walls, she was still hiding—still crouched behind the chair, still protecting herself from the pain. That little girl never left. She was still inside me.

Even as I approached thirty—believing I had finally arrived, free, healed, whole—she was still running the show. What isn't healed doesn't disappear. It simply finds ways to surface again—in the choices we make, the people we chase, the way we parent, the way we love, the way we protect, and the way we push others away.

I wasn't repeating my past on purpose. I didn't want to carry the pain forward. But without healing, we don't know how to do anything else. We live what we have learned.

I wish I could say what I learned helped me build a better life. That I broke the cycle. That I walked away and never looked back. But the truth is, I made choices rooted in pain, not healing.

I wanted love but didn't know how to recognize safety. I longed for freedom but didn't realize that trauma still held the keys.

I wanted out, but I hadn't yet healed the parts of me that kept pulling me back. And what I hadn't faced was about to show up in ways I never expected.

More than anything, I didn't want my children to carry what I had carried. I wanted them to feel safe, to know love that wasn't tangled up in fear or silence. I wanted to break the cycle for them. But you can't pass on what you've never fully received. You can't offer peace when your soul is still at war.

I love my children with everything in me. But love alone doesn't heal old wounds. It only exposes the places that still hurt. And without healing, even the best intentions can get lost in the damage we haven't faced.

For years, I had the same recurring dream: I was flying. I could feel the wind beneath me, taste freedom in the air. I was soaring, weightless, finally rising above it all. But just as I reached for the open sky, power lines appeared, thick and tangled, impossible to escape. No matter how hard I tried, I couldn't get past them. Every time, I came crashing back down.

It wasn't just a dream. It was my life. The longing to fly—to be free—was no longer just about me—it was about them. I wanted to rise so they could rise. But the power lines were still there, and I hadn't yet learned how to fly above them.

After Jatana was born, I moved back in with Jessie—my safe haven—and for once, I could breathe a little deeper and feel like my life could finally begin. My daughter was growing, a beautiful baby girl, full of life, always laughing, always curious. There was something extraordinary about her. When I looked into her eyes, it felt like she could see straight through me. I saw wisdom there, a depth far beyond her age. It wasn't just her personality. It was the gift God had placed in her. For the first time in what felt like forever, I had space to just be a mother. Not a wife trying to survive. Not a woman fighting for freedom. Just a mom. And I loved it.

Jessie was off at school, and I was in her home with my daughter, soaking in every smile, every sound, every moment of joy. The plan was simple. Once Jatana was a little older, I would go back to school and finish what I had started. I could feel my life beginning to take root, like something good was finally growing.

My son was in school, living with Maime and HB. They had stepped in to care for him in ways I couldn't at the time, and I was deeply grateful. I still saw him often. He would visit me, and I would visit him. It wasn't perfect. It wasn't what I had dreamed. But we were holding onto each other the best we could.

Then Danny took a job in Texas, and just like that, he took Little D. with him. I wasn't prepared for that kind of distance. It was hard, harder than I let anyone see. Knowing my son was hundreds of miles away and I couldn't be there tore at something deep inside me. But I had no power to stop it. I had to trust that he was safe and hold onto the small peace I had begun to build.

One day, the phone rang. It was Danny. His voice was calm, almost casual. He asked if I'd like to fly out to visit them in Texas. He said it would be a chance to see our son, and for him to see Jatana.

I felt a flicker of hope. Just to be with both of my children again, even for a little while, was all I wanted. So I said yes. But I had no idea what was waiting on the other side of that decision.

I packed our bags for what I thought would be a two-week vacation, just enough time to visit my son and let Danny see his daughter. After that, the plan was to return home and enroll in school. I was hopeful, focused, ready to move forward.

We arrived in Texas. Danny and Little D. were waiting at the airport. The moment I saw my son, he ran into my arms. He was so excited, full of joy. Then, without hesitation, he scooped up his little sister, barely a toddler, and held her like she was the best thing he had ever seen. His smile stretched across his face like everything had just been made right.

And at that moment, I felt it too. The warmth of both my children in my arms. If only for a moment, it felt whole.

Danny stood off to the side, cool and collected, hiding behind his usual calm. But I didn't care. I had my babies with me, and that was enough.

Danny had rented a small, two-bedroom apartment. It was furnished, plain, and on the second floor. It wasn't fancy, but I didn't care. I was just happy to be there with my son. Watching him play with Jatana, hearing their laughter, filled a part of me that had been empty for so long. We even went out as a family. We walked through stores and ate meals together. For a brief moment, it felt like nothing had ever gone wrong. And I let myself enjoy it. But I knew it couldn't last.

The time came to leave. I checked my flight, packed our bags, and waited for Danny to take us to the airport. He came in, saw the luggage, and picked it up. I assumed he was taking it to the truck. Instead, he walked outside, opened the back, and pulled out a ball-peen hammer.

I stood at the apartment window, frozen, as he dragged my luggage to the pavement and began to beat it with the hammer, over and over again. Then he carried what was left around the back of the building, poured gasoline on it, lit a match, and set it on fire.

I was in shock.

When he came back inside, he made it clear.

"You're not going anywhere."

His once-spoken threat echoed in my mind: *You leave me again, and I will kill you.* I was back in that prison of fear. This time, in a strange city. No family. No support. No way out. Everything I had packed, everything that represented home, freedom, and the life I was supposed to return to, was gone.

Inside, I was shaking. Rage. Fear. Confusion. All of it churned inside me like a silent scream I couldn't release. Had he planned this? Did he bring me here just to trap me again? Was it ever about the children? Or had it always been about control?

He had played the part, calm, helpful, fatherly, until the moment I tried to leave. Then he flipped the script. He didn't want me. He wanted what I gave. A caretaker. A shield. A built-in babysitter. Someone who made his life easier while he lived untouched. It wasn't love. It wasn't family. It was ownership.

Now, with no luggage, no keys, no car, the message was clear. *You're not leaving unless I say so.* What terrified me most was knowing he had probably planned it. He waited until I was there. Until I had both of my children with me. Now I had something to lose—and he knew it.

What's worse, my son saw everything. He watched his father destroy my luggage. He saw the fire, the violence, the control.

And Danny didn't flinch. No shame. No attempt to shield his child from the rage. What did that do to my son? To the boy who had just run into my arms at the airport? He didn't come for fear. He came for love. He came for family. And instead, he got this.

I stood frozen. But what was my son feeling? What happens in a child's heart when the people meant to protect him act like enemies? What does "family" become in a moment like that? Not safety. Not trust. Not love.

I wanted to reach for him, to tell him this wasn't how it was supposed to be. But the words wouldn't come. The fear was too loud. We were both frozen—two hearts breaking in the same room.

There are moments that shape us, not with tenderness, but with trauma. Watching my son witness that kind of violence broke something in both of us. I couldn't undo what he saw. And the deepest wounds are often the ones we never talk about, the ones we carry in silence. But even in that silence, God was present—not removing the pain but standing in it with us. Giving strength where there was only weakness. Holding the pieces that threatened to fall apart.

"He will cover you with his feathers, and under his wings you will find refuge; his faithfulness will be your shield and rampart."
—Psalm 91:4

There was no shield in sight that day. No one to stop the fire, the fear, or the heartbreak.

My son stood there, watching it all. In his eyes, I saw something I recognized. It was the look the girl behind the chair used to wear—wide-eyed silence. Confusion. Pain with nowhere to go.

That little girl—a younger me—had crouched behind a chair, hoping the world wouldn't see her. Now my son stood before a burning suitcase, wondering what family meant. Wondering where safety lived. I couldn't protect him from what he saw.

But Psalm 91:4 reminds me that God could. Even when we feel alone, He covers us. Even when there's no chair to hide behind, His wings become our refuge. His faithfulness doesn't always come as rescue. Sometimes, it comes as quiet strength to endure. To breathe. To survive. To keep going until healing comes. We were both wounded. But we were covered.

It wasn't until years later that I recognized that the strength I found to endure life's traumas and trials came from Him. He had been our silent protector, even in the darkest moments.

Chapter 20

Trapped, But Not Defeated

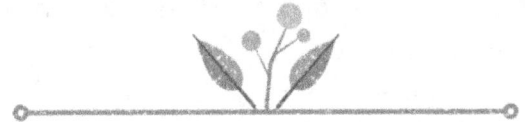

THE SMELL OF BURNING FABRIC still lingers in my memory. I can see the hammer in his hand, hear the crack of metal against my suitcase, and feel the sting of helplessness settle deep in my chest. That was the moment I knew I was trapped. Not just in Texas, but in his world again. No family. No job. No way home. My plans to return, to enroll in school, to start fresh—they all went up in flames, right there behind that apartment building. It wasn't just my luggage that burned. It was my freedom. And with it, the last sliver of hope I had that Danny might finally let me go.

The trauma of that moment didn't fade quickly. I walked around in a daze for days—going through the motions, trying to care for my children, pretending everything was fine. But I wasn't fine. I was stuck. Again. And the girl behind the chair—the one who had spent a lifetime learning how to survive—she rose up in me once more. Quiet. Numb. Alert.

The trauma wasn't mine alone. My son was unraveling too. He didn't have the words for what he was feeling, but his behavior spoke loud and clear. The little boy whose eyes once danced with joy at the sight of his family together again had started to disappear. His light dimmed. His spirit grew restless. He became angry, unpredictable, and withdrawn—a child trying to make sense of a world that had betrayed him.

And what broke me even more was that his pain began to turn toward his little sister. Maybe in his young mind, she had become the reason why his world had fallen apart. Maybe she represented the shift—the moment when his mother was no longer just his, when the family he once knew slipped out of reach. He didn't have the language to express grief, confusion, or fear. All he had was frustration, and it began to show in dangerous ways.

I couldn't stay in that place of fear. I couldn't afford to. Not with two children depending on me. I didn't have a plan, but I had a will—and sometimes, that's enough to start with.

So I did the only thing I knew how to do: I started looking for a way out. Not just a way out of Texas, but a way forward—something that would give me a sense of control, even if it was just for a few hours a day.

What came next was something unexpected. It didn't come as rescue or romance—not at first. It came as a glance. A presence. A moment I didn't ask for but couldn't ignore. I was sitting in Danny's second-story apartment, worn out from the weight of the days, staring out the window without really seeing—until I did.

And there he was. Before I could catch my breath, it hit me—a bolt of lightning straight through my chest. Sharp. Unexpected. Electric. Like nothing I had ever felt before. My body tensed, my heart raced, and for a moment, the room around me faded into the background.

He was a striking man—tall, strong, and confident. There was something magnetic about the way he moved, a presence that drew your attention and held it. His features were sharp, his look commanding, and he carried himself like someone certain of his place in the world. I didn't know his name, didn't know his story—but something in me responded before my mind had a chance to understand what I was feeling. One glance. That's all it took. And suddenly, I couldn't look away.

Shawn. He was the operations manager—not just of the complex I lived in, but of several throughout the area. This one was just one stop on his daily rounds. He wasn't there all the time, but when he was, it was impossible not to notice. He walked the grounds like he owned them—tall, composed, and confident. And tall wasn't even half of it. I had heard that everything was big in Texas—and looking at Shawn, I was starting to believe it.

He carried himself with a kind of quiet authority that didn't need to shout to be respected. The way he moved, people paid attention when he was around—he didn't just manage property, he managed presence.

He was a man with structure, with purpose, with direction. And in a season where I felt like I had none of those things, something in me took notice.

I made my way down to the leasing office, looking for work—any work. I didn't care what it was. I just needed something to help me start lifting myself back up. I needed to feel like I still had something to stand on—something solid under my feet. Because so much had been taken from me—my plans, my peace, and my power. The leasing office offered me a job cleaning the apartments after people moved out.

It wasn't glamorous, but I took it with no hesitation. Because it was mine. A small step, yes—but a real one. And at that moment, that was enough.

I put everything I had into doing a good job. Every apartment I cleaned, I treated it like it was my own. The office staff took notice—they were pleased with my work, and that gave me a small sense of pride I hadn't felt in a long time.

I started hanging around the leasing office whenever I could. I'd chat with the office manager, ask questions, and watch how things were done. I wasn't just there to clean—I wanted to learn. I picked up quickly on how things worked—how to talk to people, how to answer questions, even how to help show the apartments when someone walked in. Whatever I could do to show I was paying attention, I did it. I wanted them to see I was more than just the cleaning help—I was a quick study, and I was hungry to grow.

And they did notice. The reports made their way back to Shawn. Word got around—I worked hard, learned fast, and showed up every single day. I wasn't just cleaning apartments anymore. I was stepping into something more—and people were beginning to see it.

Then one day, Shawn came to find me. He stood in the office doorway—so tall he had to duck his head just to step through it. His presence filled the space before he even said a word. Calm, confident, steady. He looked at me—not past me, not through me, but at me. It was the kind of look that made me straighten my spine and catch my breath without even realizing it.

He spoke in a strong, deep voice—a power that shook my soul. "Would you be interested in managing one of my other properties?"

To anyone else, it might've sounded like a simple job offer. To me, it meant everything. It wasn't pity or charity—it was an open door. For the first time, I could see past the powerlines. The ones that haunted my dreams. The ones that had always stopped me mid-flight. Now, there was air beyond them—space to rise, to dream, to build a life I could call my own.

It wasn't just a job. It was a door. And I had just found the strength to walk through it.

Chapter 21

The Breaking Point

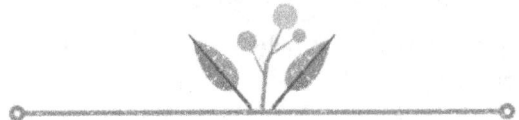

BEFORE I COULD MOVE ON to the next chapter of my life, I had to reckon with the one I was still living. Danny's control hadn't ended. He still hovered over every decision—especially when it came to the children. As much as I didn't want to be with him anymore, I knew I couldn't make this transition into a new life while leaving things in chaos. My children came first—there was never a question about that.

But having them with me meant bringing Danny too, and that was the part that tore at me. It wasn't him I wanted. It was them. But at that point in my life, keeping my family together under one roof—however fractured—felt like the only way to avoid more chaos. So I did what I believed I had to do. I accepted the cost that came with keeping my children close. It was a sacrifice—a silent one—but it allowed me to make this transition without a war. At least not yet.

It was April 4, 1982, when I stepped into my new apartment—my new job, my new life. I still carried the weight of old baggage—the threat of Danny never far behind—but for the first time, I could imagine a future that might, one day, be free of him.

I poured everything I had into learning. I wanted to succeed. I needed to. And Shawn was there to train me every step of the way. He was patient. He was kind. He never rushed me, never made me feel small. He simply guided—and I grew.

Shawn wasn't ignoring my infatuation anymore. He was a married man with children of his own. He had never made any advances toward me—he was always kind, always professional—but there was something between us neither of us could deny. It lived in the air between our words, in the pauses that lasted a second too long.

One day, he looked at me and asked, quietly but directly: "What do you want from me?" And without hesitation, I said it. "I want to taste your lips."

And then he leaned down and kissed me. I was undone. This wasn't just a kiss. It was a release. A rising. A remembering of the woman I still was beneath all the damage.

At this point in the story, I wish I could say I walked away—that I didn't let it go any further. But that wouldn't be the truth. It became an affair. One I couldn't tear myself away from. But like everything else I had tried to hold onto in the middle of chaos, it couldn't last. Danny started suspecting something. And when he feels something slipping from his grip, he does what he does best—destroys everything in his path.

Then came the night I'll never forget. I was asleep in bed with Jatana lying beside me when Danny came home from the club drunk. He walked into the room and put a .45 to my head. He pulled the hammer back. And he told me he was going to kill me.

But I wasn't afraid. Not this time. I looked him straight in the eye and said, "Go ahead. I'd rather die than keep living this lie with you." He didn't pull the trigger. He was a coward at that moment—just like he had always been when faced with my truth. He walked away. But something in me didn't.

That night gave me the courage to do what I should have done long before. I got an attorney. I filed for divorce. I was granted custody of both my children.

When Danny was served, he did what I feared most. He packed up Little D. and Jatana and drove them back to North Carolina—without my consent. And there I was. Alone in Texas. My babies were gone. Danny had taken them across state lines, across everything I had just started to rebuild.

He had always found a way to break me. But this time, I wasn't shattered. This time, I was furious. I wasn't sure how, or when, or what it would cost me—But I was going to get my children back.

Looking back now, I know the choices I made weren't perfect. I stepped into something that wasn't mine to take, and I can't excuse that. But I also know this—broken people often reach for what feels like healing, even when it's wrapped in the wrong arms.

It would take years before I understood that even in my wandering, God hadn't turned away. He was drawing me, gently, through the wilderness of my own making.

"Therefore, behold, I will allure her, will bring her into the wilderness, and speak comfort to her. I will give her her vineyards from there, and the Valley of Achor as a door of hope; She shall sing there, as in the days of her youth."

—Hosea 2:14–15 (NKJV)

Even in the wilderness of my choices, God was still calling me back—to myself, to truth, to healing, and to a door of hope I hadn't seen yet.

Chapter 22

Fighting Back

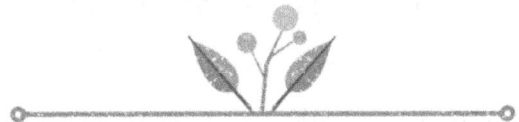

FOR SO LONG, I DREAMED OF what it would feel like to finally soar—just once—to rise above the chaos, the control, the violence. In my mind, I saw myself like a bird breaking free from the tangled wires that had always threatened to clip my wings. Those powerlines, strung tight with fear and memory, had been my ceiling. I told myself, if I can just get past them, there will be sky.

And for a moment, I did. I soared. I stood tall in my own name. I felt the wind of possibility lift me higher than I had ever been. I believed I had made it. But no one warned me what it would feel like to come crashing down.

One of those lines—thin, hidden, buried deep in my heart—reached up and struck me. The impact wasn't loud, but it was shattering. I fell—not into anyone's arms, but into the loneliness of a dream interrupted. Into the ache of missing what mattered most. I had tasted freedom, but it turned to ash the moment my children were taken from me.

I didn't waste a second. The moment the reality set in—that my children were gone—I booked a flight back to North Carolina. I had custody. I had rights. And I was going to fight for them. I called Jessie. God bless her—she met me at the airport without hesitation, no questions asked.

I knew exactly where my children were—at Maime and HB's house. I walked in believing the law was on my side. I had the official court papers from Texas in my hand, and a mother's determination in my heart. I thought I could walk in, show the documents, and take my children home. It seemed so clear. So just. But I had no idea what was waiting for me.

I entered through the side door into their small, crowded den. The moment I laid eyes on my children, everything else disappeared. I scooped my baby girl into my arms and held her tight. I could feel her warmth, her little body pressed against mine—and for a heartbeat, it felt like everything was going to be okay.

Then panic erupted. Maime ran to the phone in the hallway and dialed frantically. HB stood frozen for a split second before lunging forward. I held on to my daughter, trying to speak through the chaos—trying to tell them I had custody, that I was her mother, and I was taking my children home. But no one was listening.

In a flash, HB ripped Jatana from my arms and wrestled me to the ground like I was a criminal. He pinned me down on that thin, scratchy carpet, his weight crushing my chest while my daughter screamed for me.

Jatana was crying out, her little voice high and panicked—"Mama! Mama!"—and I couldn't even reach for her. My baby was calling for me, and I was helpless to answer.

Little D. stood in the corner of the room, just beyond the archway that led to the hallway, pressed flat against the wall. His wide eyes locked on me, frozen. I knew that look. He'd been warned by his father that I would try to take him. I saw it all in his face—confusion, fear, the heartbreaking doubt of a child unsure whether he could trust his own mother.

And still, I lay there on the floor, helpless.

Then came the sound of sirens—shrill and growing louder, cutting through the chaos like a blade. I could hear them winding down the street, closer, closer. Moments later, the front door burst open. The police stormed in, weapons at their sides, hands hovering near their holster as if I was a threat, not a mother.

HB released me, and I scrambled to my feet, breathless and shaking. I tried to collect myself, tried to look composed, but everything in me was unraveling. I grabbed my custody papers from Texas and handed them to the officers.

"I have custody," I said, my voice trembling but firm. "These are my children. I'm taking them back to Texas."

But Maime had her own set of papers—fresh, North Carolina court orders Danny had filed behind my back. While I had been surviving, healing, and fighting for my children, he had been playing the system like a well-rehearsed game. And this time, he won.

The officers looked at my documents and shook their heads. "These aren't valid here," one of them said flatly. "You'll have to take this up in Texas."

Just like that, the law crumbled beneath my feet.

They walked me to the door; I could do nothing but turn my head for one last look. Jatana was screaming for me. Danny still stood silently, his eyes tracking every move, fear and confusion locked in his small frame. And I—powerless to help either of them—was let out like an intruder in my own children's lives.

The door slammed behind me. And at that moment, standing alone in their front yard, I would've rather had that .45 go through my skull than endure the agony of leaving my babies behind.

They say, *"Hell hath no fury like a woman scorned."* But Hell had never met me.

That wasn't just a proverb anymore. It was prophecy. I was no longer a woman wounded—I was a woman enraged. A woman betrayed. And the fire that ignited in me that day could've scorched the earth. It wasn't just anger—it was fury. It was grief sharpened into a weapon. A burning, blinding rage that consumed every soft part of me and left behind something fierce, something unforgiving.

I didn't cry. I didn't beg. I didn't look back—I became *the fire*.

Chapter 23

The Cost of Survival

T HAT FIRE WOULD BURN FOR YEARS—through relationships, through courtrooms, through every lie and every betrayal. It was like an atomic bomb had gone off inside me, leveling the old version of who I was and leaving behind a survivor. A fighter. A woman who would never again be taken down without a war.

I returned to Texas without my children—but I didn't return powerless.

I knew he was back at work, moving through life like he hadn't just ripped my heart out and stomped it into the North Carolina dirt. But this time, I had something he never expected. I had the law. And I was ready to use it like a blade.

I called the police and reported him for kidnapping—taking my children across state lines without permission, violating a standing custody order. He thought he had all the power. He thought I would roll over and weep. But he didn't know who I had become.

They arrested him. And I made sure he sat in that cell and felt every minute of what he'd done. No mercy. No compassion—not this time.

He sat there in that courtroom, not the smug man who used to throw money around and bark orders. No. He looked small. Shackled at the ankles and wrists, an orange jumpsuit wrinkled around his frame, hair unkempt. His hands shook. His voice cracked as he whispered my name.

I didn't flinch.

He looked like a man unraveling—every lie, every threat, every act of cruelty folding in on him like the walls of that jail cell. Tears streamed down his face as he begged the judge for leniency, as if the tears could wash away what he'd done. He looked at me with eyes full of desperation, pleading for compassion.

But I had none left to give. Not for him.

He was guilty—not just of kidnapping. He was guilty of years of torment. Of the backseat violation that stole my innocence. Of every threat, every blow, every scar he thought I'd carry in silence. But I wasn't silent anymore. And now he would carry the weight.

They led him away in chains. And for a moment, it felt like justice.

But revenge is a strange kind of victory. It doesn't come clean. It comes with residue.

As the cell door clanged shut behind him, the fire inside me cooled just enough for me to feel something else—emptiness. The silence after the rage. The cost of holding on so tightly to pain that it begins to shape who you are.

I had won. But it didn't feel like a triumph. It felt like survival.

While Danny sat in jail, I returned to my job, trying to pick up the pieces of the life I had fought so hard to hold onto. But the atmosphere had soured—like a bouquet of roses left too long in water, the sweetness gone, the stems slimy and rotting in the vase. What once felt like a space of hope and purpose now felt strained, uncomfortable, and quietly collapsing under the weight of everything that had happened.

Shawn wanted to help. I could see it in his eyes, in the way he lingered when he spoke to me, careful with his words, but steady with his support. But his hands were tied. What I had been through—what we had shared—was no longer just private. It was messy. Complicated. And it had started to affect his life, too. His job. His reputation. To protect what he had built, he had to let me go.

But he didn't leave me stranded. Before I packed my things, Shawn made arrangements for me to take another position—in the same building where he worked. I was still in property management, still able to support myself, and still provided housing, though it was no longer in the same complex. It was a quieter role, a little more behind-the-scenes, but it kept me on my feet.

But beneath the surface, the fire still burned—lower now, like coals waiting to be stirred. I had won one battle, but the war wasn't over. My children were still gone. My heart was still raw. And I had only just begun to understand what this rage—this scorched-earth determination—was costing me.

Somehow—by some fluke, some loophole in the system I still don't understand—Danny got released from jail. One day he was locked up, and the next he was free. Free and coming to find me.

But this time, I wasn't terrified. I wasn't hiding. I wasn't begging. I was ready. Ready to fight. Ready to die—if that's what it took—for my children.

He showed up at my little apartment without warning. I opened the door, bracing for a storm, but what I saw stopped me cold. He didn't look angry—he looked worn out, like a man who had run out of road.

"I don't want to fight anymore," he said, voice low. "This is killing both of us."

"You took everything from me," I snapped. "Everything. And now you want to talk?"

He looked down, shoved his hands in his pockets. "I didn't come to start trouble. I came to find a way through this. I'll let you take Jatana."

I stared at him, heart pounding. "What do you mean, let me? She's my daughter. I have custody."

"And I'm keeping Little D.," he said firmly, meeting my eyes. "He's my son. He stays with me."

My chest tightened. "You think that's a compromise?"

"It's the best I can offer," he said. "You'll have one, I'll have one."

His words hit me like a slap.

It felt like a horse trade—cold, transactional. Like we were standing in some dusty market swapping lives instead of talking about children—our children. They weren't property to be divided. They weren't cards on a table. They were the flesh of my flesh. Pieces of my soul. And yet here we were—negotiating custody like we were bartering over livestock.

But even then, I wasn't surprised.

I remembered the night of the car chase with the waitress, when I came home shaken, afraid, and unsure of what might come next— and there he was, lying on the floor next to Little D.'s crib. Not waiting for me. Not protecting me, but watching over him. That was when I first truly understood—it was never about me. It was always about his son.

Even when I escaped to New Jersey and he tracked me down, brought me back against my will—I see it now—that, too, was about his son. About not losing him. About keeping hold of the one thing that gave him a sense of power, of identity, of legacy. Whether he knew how to be a father or not, Little D. was the most important thing in his life.

And at that moment, I flashed back to the night HB held me down on the floor and the police stormed in. I could still see my son standing in the doorway, pressed against the wall—terrified. Not of strangers. Not of the chaos. But of me. His mother.

Because his father had made me a threat in his eyes.

Danny had made that little boy his idol. His image. His legacy. And no matter what I felt about the man, he loved his son. In his own broken, possessive, twisted way—he loved him. And my son loved him back.

I hated it. I hated the weight of that truth. But I couldn't deny it.

I could fight, yes. I could tear everything apart trying to take Little D. back. But at what cost? What would that do to him? To both of them? To me? At that moment, I knew what I had to do.

I had my baby girl to consider as well. Jatana had already begun to feel the weight of it—her brother's confusion, his divided loyalty, and his rage, even if he didn't understand it. The unspoken, inherited anger had started showing up in how he treated her. She had become the quiet target of what none of us knew how to fix.

Maybe I was trying to rationalize it—to find some way to make peace with what I was about to do. Maybe it was just me trying to survive another impossible choice.

But I did it—I let him go.

And in doing so, I gave up a piece of myself I'll never get back. There's no way to describe what it feels like to release your own child—not because you don't love him, but because you do. Because somewhere deep inside, you believe it's the only way to save all of you.

It didn't feel brave. It didn't feel right. It just felt *necessary*.

For a long time, I carried shame for that decision. I questioned it. I turned it over again and again in the dark, wondering if I had failed him—or if I had finally found strength to surrender what I couldn't save.

But even in that place of brokenness, something gentle stirred in me. Not forgiveness, not yet. But a whisper of understanding. Of mercy. A reminder that I was never walking alone.

"He heals the brokenhearted and binds up their wounds."
—Psalm 147:3

That verse wrapped around me like a comforting blanket in a cold season. I wasn't healed yet, but I was held. And sometimes, that was enough to get through the night.

Chapter 24

The Beginning of Redemption

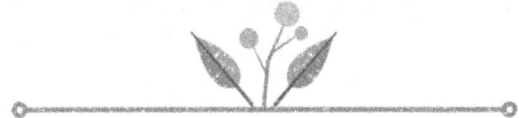

DANNY AND I DROVE BACK TO North Carolina together—not out of love, but exhaustion. Maybe we had just run out of fight. I picked up Jatana, hugged my son goodbye, and walked out of that house. It wasn't fair, but it was final.

Jessie came with me back to Texas and stayed a while to help me get back on my feet but then went back to North Carolina. Shawn arranged for me to have my own apartment again, with the model home right next door. It gave us rhythm and security—but I was still missing my son.

Texas had been a battleground. I hadn't won every fight, but I had survived. And sometimes, surviving is enough. Still, it was never home. I had no family there. Just a job, a few quiet allies, and the ghosts of everything I'd endured.

I was tired of being alone. Tired of being strong every single day. I missed my son. So I packed our things and returned to North Carolina.

Jessie welcomed us into her home again without hesitation. I enrolled back in school and picked up part-time work as a substitute teacher. During the day, I filled in wherever I was needed. At night, I studied—exhausted, but determined. Jessie stayed home with Jatana so I could focus.

As I began rebuilding, I reconnected with my family. My sister Betty had two daughters and was working in retail. She had taken a steady, faithful path that looked nothing like mine but still felt like home. My brother Gary had built a successful HVAC business and had two kids of his own. Even my oldest brother, Charles, who lived in Memphis, remained a thread in the fabric of where I came from. After my father's death, my mother remarried. My relationship with her was distant, but I was learning to make peace with that too.

One day, Jessie and I drove to Florida to visit my dear friend Kara. The moment we saw each other, it was as if no time had passed. I told her everything—my story, the wounds, the small victories. She listened with that same steady heart she'd always had. Then she asked, "Would you want to come live with us for a while?"

I hadn't expected that, but I recognized God opening a door I hadn't even knocked on. So after finishing my semester, I packed up, loaded Jatana into the car, and we moved to Florida.

Kara didn't just welcome us—she embraced us. She became like a mother to Jatana, loving her like she was her own. For the first time in a long time, we felt safe, supported, and seen.

I soon found a property management job in Jacksonville. It came with an apartment, and we began building a life of our own. Sometimes Danny would visit; sometimes I'd drive back to North Carolina for the holidays. Those visits with my son meant everything. Despite all we had been through, *love had survived.*

While living in Jacksonville, I enrolled in real estate school. I didn't know exactly where the path would lead, but I needed options—something that could give me control over my future. Earning that license would open doors later.

When Kara's husband was transferred to Orlando, they moved to a town nearby. I didn't want to be far from her, so I looked for work in the area and found another property management job—that's where I met Robert.

He was older, quiet, and kind—the facilities assistant at the property. Every morning, he'd bring me coffee and something to eat. It wasn't flashy. It was steady. And after everything I had lived through, that kind of quiet consistency meant something.

I wasn't looking for love. But Robert's gentleness caught my attention—and eventually, my heart. We moved in together and began a life of our own. I was selling real estate. He worked in logistics. It wasn't a fairytale, but it was real. For the first time, I felt like I was building a life—not just surviving one.

Robert's adopted mother was known as Miss Hallelujah. She was a woman of faith. When she found out her son was living with a woman, she didn't scold me. She prayed.

And something began to shift.

I used to mock people like her—"holy rollers," I called them. But now, it felt like Jesus was everywhere. Not with guilt or shame—but with grace. With presence. With persistence. And something inside me began to stir.

One day, I took Jatana to the playground. As I sat on a bench, a woman approached. She didn't look like a preacher, but I knew—she was one of them. I braced myself for the conversation, but she was kind. We talked about motherhood, hardships, and hope. Just as she was about to leave, she reached for my hand and said, "Let's pray."

Right there on the playground, she bowed her head and prayed out loud. I didn't close my eyes. I didn't know what to do. But something in her words pierced me.

That night, I went home and stared at the marijuana plant I had been growing. Without hesitation, I pulled it up by the roots and took it outside to the trash. Then I knelt down and whispered, *"God... if You're real, I want to know You."*

No fancy prayer. No preacher. Just me and God.

From that moment on, everything began to change.

I started going to church with Miss Hallelujah. I couldn't get enough. I read the Bible like it was water for a thirsty soul—from Genesis to Revelation. And I found a God who was not distant or passive, but fierce and near. A God who pursued the broken and made them whole.

Not long after, Lillian—an old friend from my party days—came to visit. I was nervous. I wasn't that woman anymore. But as soon as she walked in, I saw it—she had changed too. God had gotten hold of her as well. We rejoiced, prayed, and reconnected in the Light.

Before she left, she invited me to a prayer meeting and I promised I'd go.

That Christmas, I drove to North Carolina to spend time with my son. While I was there, I went with Lillian to the prayer meeting. I didn't know what to expect—but what I experienced changed me forever.

The power of God came upon me so strongly I couldn't even stand. I fell to the floor—laughing, crying, overwhelmed. It felt like years of pain were being pulled from the deepest places in me. Love, healing, and freedom flooded my soul.

When it was over, only a few people remained in the room. But I was not the same woman who had walked in. Something had lifted. I saw the world differently. I loved everyone. Even the air felt different—I had encountered the living God.

Driving back to Florida with Jatana, I was filled with a joy too deep for words. I told Miss Hallelujah everything. She just smiled. She had been praying for it all along.

I had searched for so long—for peace, for safety, for love. And in one holy moment, I found it all—in Him. I discovered that Jesus isn't just a story. He is alive. And He had come for me. I wasn't just turning a new page. I was living in a brand-new book.

"Therefore, if anyone is in Christ, he is a new creation. The old has passed away: behold, the new has come."

—2 Corinthians 5:17

In Christ, I didn't just find forgiveness; I became new—washed, whole, and truly free.

Chapter 25

The Call

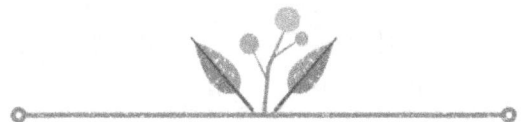

I N 1985, AFTER MY DIVORCE FROM Danny was finalized, I married Robert. We settled into a small home outside of Orlando, Florida. It wasn't extravagant, but it was peaceful. We had found steady work, Jatana was in preschool, and I had discovered a small country church where I could continue growing in my faith. Life felt grounded, simple, and full of quiet hope.

One afternoon, I was sitting on my bedroom floor, praying quietly, when I heard something that stopped me cold. *"I am sending you to the nations."*

The voice was unmistakable. It wasn't loud, but it was clear. My only response was, "Lord, how can I go to the nations? I have a small child."

And He answered just as clearly: *"Who do you think gave you that child? And don't you think I can take care of her?"*

I had no defense. No words. Just awe and confusion. But like Jonah, I ran—not toward the call, but from it. I chose safety. I built a life that looked responsible, stable, and manageable. I told myself I was being wise, but in truth, I was afraid.

Still, God didn't forget.

He wasn't after my hustle. He was after my heart. And little by little, He began to strip away the things I had relied on—my confidence, my plans, my illusions of control. Not to harm me, but to heal me.

God began to deal with me—not the version I showed the world, but the real me. The girl behind the chair. The one who had survived abuse, betrayal, abandonment, and had learned to serve while bleeding. She was strong, yes—but she had never been whole. And now, God was calling her out. Not to shame her, but to heal her.

Before I could carry His message to the world, I had to let Him carry mine. It began with the one thing I had buried deepest: *"You must forgive your father."*

I was furious. How could God ask that of me? How could He expect me to forgive a man who had abused me, who had scarred me, who never once made it right?

But then I had a dream. In the dream, I was in heaven. My father was there, peaceful and gentle. He walked beside me, pointing to things and speaking with childlike joy. Then he turned to me and said, "Cindy, would you forgive me for all the things I did to you?"

I woke up stunned, shaken. But something in me had shifted. Somehow, in the mystery of God's grace, my father had called on the name of the Lord before he died—and God had received him. Not because he deserved it, but because that's who God is.

It didn't erase the damage, but it freed me from the bitterness I'd carried for years. That forgiveness was never for him—it was for me. So I forgave him. And my heart was set free.

But God wasn't finished.

At a Christian retreat, as I lay in bed, I had a sudden image of my mother's face. It hit me like lightning. A dam broke inside, and I began to weep with an anguish I hadn't known was still there. At that moment, I realized something painful: I couldn't remember her ever telling me she loved me. I couldn't remember her being there. She hadn't protected me. And deep down, I had hidden the truth—I hated her. I had masked it with excuses, buried it in indifference. But God was pulling it into the light.

The next day, I called her. I told her everything. The memory, the grief, the pain I had carried. And to my surprise, she wept. "I didn't know," she said. "I'm so sorry." I didn't know if it was the truth or just comfort. But I knew this: I was ready to forgive her. And when I did, something in both of us changed.

She asked me about my faith—about the God who was doing this work in me. Through tears, I led her in a prayer of salvation right there on the phone. It wasn't perfect, but it was real. That moment didn't erase the past. But it rewrote our future.

God gave me compassion for the woman I had once only seen through the lens of pain. And my heart began to soften. Forgiveness didn't bring answers. But it brought freedom—the kind that breaks chains and rebuilds hearts. God was giving me a new heart, just as He promised in Ezekiel 36:26, *"I will remove your heart of stone and give you a heart of flesh"* (CSB).

For the first time, I wasn't just surviving the pain. I was healing from it. And healing led to deeper trust. God wasn't just calling me to believe—He was calling me to walk with Him.

One verse echoed in my spirit: *"I am the way, the truth, and the life"* (John 14:6, NKJV).

I had read it before. But now it became alive to me. Jesus wasn't pointing to the way. He *was* the Way. He wasn't speaking about truth. He *was* Truth. He didn't offer life. He *was* Life.

And that was the beginning. The beginning of surrender. The beginning of purpose. The beginning of a life no longer running from the call but preparing to answer it.

Chapter 26

The Long Road Home

MAYBE THIS ISN'T THE CHAPTER readers expect next. Because this isn't where I fought, ran, or rose. This is where I wandered—again.

For twenty years, I ran from the calling I knew was mine. I still loved God, still believed, but I put Him on a shelf—quietly ignored while I tried to build my own life. I was raising my daughter, working, surviving. But inside, I was dry.

I had forgiven my father and mother, thinking that was enough. But healing takes more than forgiveness. It takes honesty, courage, and a willingness to face what you've hidden even from yourself.

Robert, my second husband, was kind and steady, but he carried the weight of wounds he hadn't caused. We moved to Arizona, which was supposed to be a fresh start, but its desert heat only mirrored the dryness in my soul. Our marriage withered, and I returned to North Carolina with Jatana, carrying more baggage in my heart than in my hands.

That's when I reconnected with Lillian and met her brother, Brian. He came with charm and trouble in equal measure. We settled along the coast in North Carolina, just before Hurricane Hugo slammed the coast. The storm tore apart homes, streets, and lives—and in many ways, it mirrored my own.

Brian and I married in 1991 on a stormy March day. The winds roared, the ceremony moved indoors, and a slammed door punctuated our vows. I didn't listen to the warning in it. Brian was generous but battled alcohol, drugs, and infidelity. And in marrying him, I had brought my daughter into a life I swore I'd never repeat.

Ten years passed. Then came September 11, 2001. Jatana was on her way to college when she called. "Mom, did you hear? A plane hit the Twin Towers." I turned on the radio and listened as both towers fell. With them, something inside me collapsed.

For years, I had built a life out of survival—strong on the outside, hollow at the core. That day, the walls came down. I hit my knees and surrendered: *"I'll go where You send me. I'll do whatever You say."*

Two towers fell in New York, and the last of my resistance fell with them. Everything I had built apart from God crumbled, but in the rubble, I saw the beginning of something real. The following verse became my promise:

"Those from among you shall build the old waste places; you shall raise up the foundations of many generations; and you shall be called the Repairer of the Breach."

—Isaiah 58:12 (NKJV)

God wasn't just calling me to be healed—He was calling me to rebuild. Nothing in my life had to be wasted. Even my ruins could become a road for someone else to find their way home.

Chapter 27

The Release

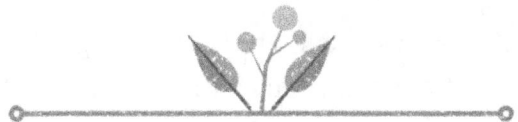

JANUARY 1, 2005, WAS A DAY OF celebration—bright with joy and promise—but also sacred. As I stood in the sanctuary waiting for my daughter to walk down the aisle, a quiet wave of reflection swept over me. My heart was full—not just because of what was unfolding before me, but because of everything that had led there.

My eyes found my son among the groomsmen—tall, steady, confident. And for a moment, I didn't just see the man he had become. I saw the little boy who had once clung to me through chaos, the teenager who wrestled with more than he should've, the young man who rose up from brokenness with quiet strength.

His journey hadn't been easy. There were wounds he never deserved to carry—but by the grace of God, he made it through. He didn't just survive—he grew into a man of honor, a faithful husband, and a loving father.

When I watched him hold his own son, David, for the first time, something shifted in me. I saw gentleness in his hands, legacy in his eyes. And as I cradled my grandson, I heard the Lord whisper, *"The chain ends here."* That moment marked the beginning of healing—for him, for me, and for the generations to come.

Then, my eyes moved from my son to the man at the altar—Joshua—the groom, the one waiting for my daughter. He stood composed, his gaze fixed on the back of the sanctuary, anticipation in every breath. I didn't just see a man in a tuxedo. I saw the answer to years of prayer. The promise of God, standing in flesh and bone, waiting to receive the treasure He had entrusted to me.

Joshua wasn't just a good man. He was a godly man—quiet in strength, steady in conviction. He carried the faith of Abraham, the leadership of Moses, the strength of Samson, and the heart of David. I had prayed for a man like him—through tears, through uncertainty, through long nights when I didn't know how the story would turn out. And here he was, standing at the altar, eyes full of love. He adored her—I could see it.

And then, the sanctuary fell silent. The doors opened—not to the sound of the usual bridal march, but something deeper. "Jesus Loves Me" played softly and slowly, pure in tone, and full of weight.

My breath caught. There she was—my daughter, Jatana. Dressed in white. Glowing. She looked fragile in beauty but fierce in spirit—a real-life princess stepping into her promise.

And beside her... was her father. At that moment, something sacred happened inside me.

I didn't see the man who had hurt me. I didn't see the one who once tried to take my children from me. I saw the Father. The One who, in His mercy, had chosen to give me my two greatest gifts through this man.

There was no bitterness. No sting of the past. Only gratitude. Because through him, God had entrusted me with my son—now standing tall with quiet strength—and my daughter, walking with grace toward her future.

"Jesus loves me, this I know…" It wasn't just a sweet melody from childhood. It was a declaration. A banner. A holy anthem sung over two lives built not on tradition, but on truth.

They weren't just making vows—they were making covenants. Their love story had been shaped by prayer, surrender, and faith. And now, they were choosing to build on a foundation that would not fail. The same Jesus who loved them as individuals would now stand at the center of their union.

Each step she took whispered grace. Each note of that song echoed healing. And as I watched, I heard God's words again: *"Don't you think I can take care of her?"*

And He had. He had protected her in ways I never could. He had shaped her into a woman of dignity, faith, and strength. And in her surrender, I found my own.

Twenty years had passed since I first heard Him whisper, *"I'm sending you to the nations."* For years, I resisted—fearing she needed me more than the world ever could. But now I knew: she was in His hands. She was ready. And at last, so was I.

Everything I once clung to in fear, I released in love. And in that holy moment, my heart whispered back: *"I gave her to You, Lord. Now take me wherever You will."*

Chapter 28

To the Ends of the Earth

THE CHURCH I HAD BEGUN ATTENDING was deeply rooted in missions. It wasn't just something they supported—it was who they were. They believed in going, in sending, in reaching the ends of the earth with the love of Christ. And before long, that heartbeat became mine.

When a ministry from India visited, I had no idea it would mark the beginning of everything God had been preparing me for. They showed photos of orphaned children, spoke of feeding programs, and shared how water wells opened doors in unreached villages. I was stirred—deeply. I had heard the call before, but now, I was finally ready to respond.

I volunteered for the next trip. God confirmed my decision in personal, intimate ways—including sending another woman on the trip in answer to my prayer not to go alone. I wasn't going because I was brave. I was going because I was willing.

That trip to India changed everything. The poverty shocked me. The heat was relentless. The culture, unfamiliar. But amidst the chaos and exhaustion, I saw the Gospel alive. We traveled from village to village, offering food, clothing, and prayers. And I witnessed my first miracle—a little boy with polio walking for the first time after prayer. I came to serve, but it was my own faith that was transformed.

After the mission trip, I thought I would return to life as usual. I couldn't. My heart had changed. I had changed.

Later, I traveled to Kenya, where I served as the temporary overseer of an orphanage in Bungoma. The orphanage sat nestled in a mountainous region, surrounded by green beauty. When I arrived, the children greeted me with welcome signs and hugs. I was overwhelmed by their joy and by the weight of responsibility. The compound had buildings for the children, a guard house, a bookkeeper's office, a small cottage for me, and a partially completed structure. A playground stood at the center, a symbol of childhood amid hardship.

I oversaw daily needs, led devotionals, and uncovered corruption in the organization. When a threat came against my life, a missionary named Scott intervened and helped me return safely. But my heart remained in Africa. I later went back and studied under Scott at a Bible college in Bungoma.

After Kenya, I traveled to the Czech Republic and Ukraine, where I witnessed a post-communist culture hungry for love. I gave out free hugs in city squares and prayed with those who had never heard the name of Jesus spoken in kindness.

Eventually, I returned to the U.S., weary but full. I lived with my daughter in Virginia and waited on God for where He would send me next.

That's when Hope House in Manassas became part of my story. While living there, I poured myself into caring for others, offering encouragement, structure, and love. It was there I met Jim and Marianne—gentle, generous people who opened their home to me when my time at the Hope House ended. The Lord told them to prepare a room just for me, and I moved in with a sense of gratitude and wonder.

Their home became a place of deep healing. I found joy in the quiet, peace in the routines, and fellowship in our conversations. It was a gift I didn't expect but one that I received with open hands and a surrendered heart.

"The Lord directs the steps of the godly. He delights in every detail of their lives." —Psalm 37:23 (NLT)

From India to Kenya, from Europe to Virginia—every step, every story, led me to where I am now.

Chapter 29

The Girl Steps Out

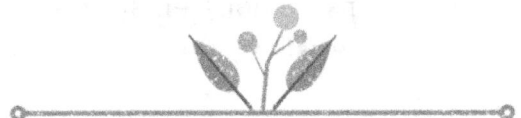

J IM AND MARIANNE'S INVITATION to stay in their home wasn't just an act of kindness—it was a divine appointment. It reminded me of Elijah, taken in and given a place to rest so he could be renewed for what was ahead.

During the past three years, while living with them, I've reflected deeply on my life's journey—on what it all meant, and why healing was still needed from the trauma of my childhood. Marianne began meeting with me one-on-one, walking me through the steps of identifying the hidden wounds that still had influence over my life. We addressed forgiveness—my father, my mother, and the men who had hurt me.

I came to see something I had never realized before: we can serve God with our gifts, love people deeply, and still feel empty inside without understanding why. That emptiness comes when we've never allowed God to touch the deepest parts of our hearts, where true healing and life begin.

The mind can rationalize anything, but the heart tells the truth—whether it cries out loudly or stays silent. God's Word reminds us: *"Above all else, guard your heart, for everything you do flows from it"* (Proverbs 4:23).

Even science confirms what Scripture has been saying all along. The heart isn't just a pump—it has its own "little brain," a complex network of about 40,000 neurons that process information and send more signals to the brain than the brain sends back. This means the heart doesn't just receive instructions—it speaks. It influences our thoughts, emotions, and decisions, often before we consciously realize it.

That's why God focuses on the heart. It's where truth is held, where wounds are buried, and where healing must begin. When the heart is whole, it sends life-giving signals to the mind, shaping how we think, what we feel, and how we live. But when it's broken or guarded by walls, it can keep us from fully experiencing the abundant life Jesus promised.

Marianne didn't just speak to my head; she ministered to my heart. As we worked through those hidden places, I became more alive than ever before—more hungry for the depth of who God created me to be.

Unexpectedly, my sister Betty died. Suddenly, it was as if everything I had gained came crashing down. I couldn't understand why. In our sessions, we discovered that I had unknowingly made Betty my protector instead of the Lord. I repented, but something still felt blocked—like a door I couldn't get open.

I had always been told, through religious teaching, that a Christian cannot have a demon. I'm not here to debate theology—but I am here to tell you what the Lord showed me. The "girl behind the chair" still carried hidden pain—rejection, loss, and the silencing of my voice.

During one small home fellowship, six of us gathered—Jim, Marianne, me, and three others. I told them about this wall I felt inside—one I couldn't seem to break through, no matter how hard I tried. I asked for prayer. I told the Lord, "I want this wall down, no matter what it is or what I have to do. I am willing, Lord."

Then Jim said, "Lord, how do You see Cindy?" Instantly, something began to stir deep inside me—a weight, an agony, that I couldn't explain. A groaning rose from deep within me, and I screamed, *"Hell has no fury like a woman scorned."*

When I said those words, it was as if the deep agony from all that I had lived through surged upward and came out of me. What happened next felt like breaking through the surface of water after being submerged too long. I gasped, my lungs filling—not with ordinary air, but with life-giving breath from Heaven. At that moment, I was free.

My life began to play before me like a movie on a screen—every hidden thing brought into the light. The little girl who hid behind the chair for so long finally stepped out—whole and complete. Not in my own strength, but in the fullness of who God is in me, and what He has revealed through me. God wants nothing hidden.

The freedom I experienced opened the door for me to write this book. I share this story for one simple reason: I pray it encourages others to step out of the shadows of their past. If you have known trauma, brokenness, or pain, allow the Lord to reveal what is hidden, heal what is broken, and lead you into the freedom He died to give. To live the abundant life is to live with peace in your heart, joy unspeakable, and the unshakable trust that God holds you—no matter what comes.

This is my story—my redemption story. And I have learned that *forgiveness is the key that unlocks the Kingdom of God.*

Epilogue

WHAT BEGAN AS A STORY of survival became a journey of surrender. And surrender became the open door to a life I never imagined.

For years, I carried the weight of what was broken—the shame, the silence, and the wounds that shaped the girl behind the chair. Even as I served God and obeyed His call to go to the nations, parts of my heart were still bound. I loved Him deeply, but I did not yet see myself the way He saw me.

I went in faith—broken, but willing. And He used even my brokenness to touch others. From the dusty villages of India to the green hills of Kenya, from the cobblestone streets of the Czech Republic to the resilient hearts of Ukraine, I witnessed miracles of His mercy. I saw the hungry fed, the lost found, and the hopeless restored. Yet even as I carried His message of freedom to others, there were chains within me still waiting to fall.

Then came the day of deliverance—the day heaven touched earth in my heart. In that sacred moment, my eyes were opened, and I finally saw myself as He had seen me all along: not as the girl who had survived, but as His beloved daughter, completely free. That day changed everything. The striving ceased, and the peace I had preached to others finally became my own.

That was the moment true healing began—the day I stopped living for Him out of duty and began living with Him out of love. Freedom came not from the nations I reached, but from the revelation of who I am in Him.

Those stories—the missions, the miracles, and the message of that final freedom—will be told in time. For now, this book closes where every true beginning starts: at the feet of Jesus, where the girl behind the chair finally found her freedom.

✳ · ✳ · ✳

The chair is empty now. The girl who once hid there walks free—her head lifted, her heart whole, her steps steady in the light of the One who called her out.

Her journey continues—not to find herself, but to reveal the One who found her.

"For you died, and your life is now hidden with Christ in God."
—Colossians 3:3

Hidden in Him—there is no need to prove, perform, or be seen. Only to follow, to love, and to walk in the freedom He has already given.

Declaration of Surrender and Freedom

T HIS IS A SEASON TO WALK unashamed and unapologetic in the path prepared by God alone.

The Girl Behind the Chair is more than a book—it is a testimony of the One who brings us out of hiding and into His marvelous light. The story ends where true life begins: when the girl steps out from behind the chair and into the freedom purchased by Jesus Christ, restoring what was lost and reconciling us to our Heavenly Father.

This journey is not about striving, but surrender; not about rising higher, but bowing lower. It is the letting go of every weight, every distraction, and every tie that does not lead to holiness.

All glory belongs to the One who calls, redeems, and restores.

About the Author

C INDY HUNT IS THE PROUD MOTHER of two and grandmother of four. After many years of traveling the world on mission work in places such as Kenya, India, the Czech Republic, and Ukraine, she has recently relocated back to South Carolina. Now resting in God's redeeming love, Cindy is embracing a new season of peace and purpose. She is currently preparing to write her next book, which will chronicle her missionary journeys and the life-changing lessons of faith, healing, and surrender she discovered along the way.

KINGDOM BRIDGES
PUBLISHING

 Check out our projects at: kingdombn.com/publishing

 Find us on Socials @Kingdombn

 Find us on Streaming @Kingdombn